COPYRIGHT

The Mind of Student

First Edition

Copyright © 2016 by Allen Olatunde

+2348032346674

ISBN: 978-9-785-08925-7

Africa! GLOW Missions Connect, Abeokuta, Nigeria

Block 2, Baptist Quarters, Idi-Aba, Abeokuta, Ogun State, Nigeria.

TABLE OF CONTENTS

DEDICATION

To All Teenagers Who had Passed Through My Hands And To All Students Who Are Creative And Innovative I Dedicate.

This Book and to My Sons and Daughters: Caleb Dantala Tanko, Alice Mary Offiono, Bukola Adesina, Emmanuel Adesina, Emmanuel Omotoso, Favour Omotoso, Nathaniel Oladele, Testimony Olajire, Peace Olabiyi, Stephen Fakorede, Stella Ogundairo, Femi Emmanuel Ojo, Qudus Bello, Motunrayo Ogunriande, Philips Olatunde, MofopeAlabi and Surprise Vaughan.

ACKNOWLEDGEMENT

To God who created man and his mind, be the glory for the great things He did for mankind.

I am glad to express a profound appreciation to Rev. Dr. S.A.K. Olaleye, the Director of Youth and Student Ministry of Nigerian Baptist Convention, who painstakingly read through the book to write foreword. May God bless you sir.

I acknowledge my fathers in the Lord who guide, encourage and has influenced me in the work of the ministry: Rev. Dr. Paul O. Kolawole, President, Osun Baptist Conference, Osogbo; Rev. (Evang.) Olufela Adenmosun, Chrtogm, London; Rev. Dr. A. A. Alade (Rtd), Gateway B.C., Ibadan; Rev. Banjo Ajao, First B.C., Kaduna; Rev. E. Adedeji, Gateway B.C., Ibadan; Rev. Prof. 'Deji Ayegboyin, Head of Religious Studies Department, University of Ibadan, Ibadan; Rev. Dr. Ezekiel Bamigboye (Rtd), NBTS, Ogbomoso; Rev. Dr. Moses Audi, Baptist Theological Seminary, Kaduna; Rev. M. O. Abayowa, Zion B.C., Minna; Rev. Olufemi Oyekan, New Height B.C., Port Harcourt; Rev. Dr. Wale Olajire, Antioch B.C., Ogbomoso; Rev. Gideon Akanbi, President, Godly Brain, Ibadan; Rev. Dr. Femi Adewumi, Director of Global Missions Board of NBC, Ibadan; and Prof. Ademola Ajayi, Head of History Department, University of Ibadan, Ibadan.

Special thanks to my brethren, friends and loved ones whom God used to painstakingly read through the book and also financially support the work. May God honour your input and use this book to bless lives as your hearts desire. I cannot appreciate you enough. Thanks a million.

Temitayo Olatunde, my closest friend, my wife, whose belief in me and tireless efforts of support are helping many of my dreams come true.

Darasimi, Jemimah and Alice, who provide daily support at home during the compilation of this book. I will always appreciate you. I believe also in your innovative future.

I also thank my parent, Engr (Late) Edward and Mrs. Florence Olatunde, for giving me opportunity to go to school, created learning environment for me and also support my vision. To my siblings, thanks for being there.

Thanks to the proprietor of Patterson Memorial Baptist Grammar School and President, Ogun Baptist Conference, Rev. DrA.B. Jayesimi and the school community who provide environment for ministry.

Young adults of Antioch Baptist Church, Ogbomoso and Zion Baptist Church, Minna, whose unwavering confidence in my ministry is appreciated. I appreciated the environment you created for me.

Thanks to all students of Patterson Memorial Baptist Grammar School, Abeokuta, who believe in my chaplaincy and innovative dream. Your questions and 'want to know' acts gave birth to this great work. I love you all.

FOREWORD

Wao!!! This is classic. Here is a book well written to address something very crucial to Youth and Student Ministry. Are you working with the Youth? Are you ministering to teenagers and students? You need to know The Mind of Student. One major reason why many of us in Youth and Student Ministry often mishandle our assignment is because we lack understanding of the mind of the generation we are mandated to minister to. While our brain is focusing on the right side, our "congregation" is thinking to the left. We wonder why these young people would not understand and obey simple instructions while they wonder why we are "misbehaving" and we cannot see "reality" from their own perspective. We want them to behave normal at this stage but Anna Frend says "to be normal during the adolescent period is by itself abnormal." The generation gap is getting widened because we have not taken a conscious effort to study the operation of the mind of our target audience. This is a major reason we are losing this generation of people to other contending forces outside the church.

The Mind of Student is not just a book for student workers; it is also a useful material for students themselves. Many students are confused and take rash decisions they later regret in life. Majority of the youths cannot explain the reasons for their decisions because their minds work so fast and react so quickly to their environment to the point that they take a short time to think and disregard many factors before they rush into action. Many have been displaced today because of the wrong actions they took yesterday. With this book, young folks can have a better understanding of the working of their minds so as to take right decision at this stage for future fruitful life.

Brother Allen Olatunde has done a very good work in putting this material together. This is one of the best books I have seen on teenage/student/youth ministry. This is a well-researched material that goes to the depth of the subject. A lot of issues are considered here that can help both teenagers/students/youths on one hand and their ministers/parents on the other hand. The author has done a proper diagnosis of the mind of students. Everyone with the mindset of winning this young generation will find this book a useful tool for their ministry.

I appreciate the painstaking effort this writer has put in the production of this book. He has done a very good work. I hereby commend this book to all who desire to have relevant and effective ministry to the teenagers, students and youths of this generation. This is a material you need. I also encourage every youth especially students to go through and digest this material for life application. You will gain a lot, I promise you.

Above all I pray that the Holy Spirit will interpret the content of this book into the hearts of the readers so that these written words might become instruments of transformation to their minds. May you be blessed of the Lord as you go through this material in Jesus' name.

Rev. Dr. S.A.K. Olaleye

Director of Youth and Student Ministry,

Nigerian Baptist Convention,

October, 2016

PREFACE

On the day I finished the printing of my second book, Career Choice Made Easy, I perceived within myself the title of next book which is now a reality, The Mind of Student. Many issues filled my mind on what, why and how to write this book to address the challenges and distractions that daily affect studentship in Africa, nevertheless, God saw me through. The Mind of Student came as a result of observations I had whenever I was privileged to sit around students. I saw challenges of internal wars and external disturbances which led to mass failure, truancy, purposeless living, thuggery, rape, unemployment, joblessness, academic death and loss of future dream. I believe that all students can perform very well in any examination if the mind is sound. Many worries and noises come to the mind within the school environment and outside her fence. All these affect reading and studying.

Moreover, if a patient knows what is wrong with him, the doctor's work is simple. Most students have unidentified and undefined problems. I learnt that students are just entering campuses just to collect certificate without thorough learning, conscious reading and innovative studying. They are curious to finish to get exposed to fun, sex, etc. They fail exam woefully and lose interest in schooling because of problems associated to students' mind such as: problem of assimilation, health tussle, financial interruption, excuses, etc. All these issues are systematically addressed in this book.

Again, the rate of excellent performance in schools today has dropped because of the distractions that depress the mind. Students want to get rich, popular, attractive, and impressive yet without following due process of learning. The ugly pictures of our leaders and celebrities had corrupted the mind of students from schooling; they also want quick fame, power and ungodly wealth at all cost. Studentship is not for wealth accumulation but to solve problems. Many students do not have future target - dream. Dream is the in-built drive for learning. If the dream is affected negatively, the passion to study will drop. What do you aim to save, discover or produce in the future for other generation to benefit from? This question is my reason for this book. I wish Nigerian students could realize how blessed we are in the world. If you do not face your studies now, poverty in Africa will not just remain but daily increase for your unborn children. Africans are major consumers of new discoveries of other nations. Why? Their students were empowered for commercialized innovation. Only the serious students would benefit from such empowerment. History, for decades, only maintains the names of past heroes of inventions and discoveries. What will you do to replace the heroes with new invention, discoveries, principles, ideas or theories that will place Nigeria in the best place in the world? You can be the latest inventors if you bend low to learn purposefully without distractions that will not feed or clothe you for life. This book guides the students to understand the great reservoir, God deposited in man - THE MIND. Your mind has capacity to discover solution to any problem you perceive as you school. This book will engage your mind for possibilities.

The book actually draws students' attention to God as the Initiator of all ideas. If you read prayerfully, you will be a step further to your dream. As you read, prepare to change some distracting acts for innovative values. Write down your dreams and strategically study to achieve them as you depend on God for strength. Ideas are stocked in your mind. You can be great if you believe you can.

Please take note: This book is not an oriental way of acquiring knowledge or abstract travel. It is the God's way of complementing your reading effort as student. What you read is what you think through for better implementation as you achieve your dream. Bible talks about 'renewing your mind' (Romans 12:2; Eph. 4:23), 'loving God with all our mind' (Mark 12:30), and Paul also pray for us that "Let this mind be in you which was also in Christ Jesus' (Phil. 2:5). Our mind is not the all-in-all for creativity, it has root in God' ability. Thinking without God is not biblical. So, think along and with God.

Allen Olatunde
August, 2016

CHAPTER ONE

THE MIND OF STUDENT

Learning is not attained by chance; it must be sought for with ardor and attended to with diligence – Abigail Adams

In youth we learn, in age we understand – Marie Von Ebner

Who is a student? A student in the eye of everyone is a learner and everyone who tries to get knowledge in order to solve problems in the immediate and global environment is also a student. It can be seen in two ways according to Microsoft Encarta Dictionary[i] that student is a person studying (somebody who studies at a school, college, or university) and a knowledgeable or interested person (somebody who has studied or takes much interest in a particular subject). It can also be called a scholar, pupil, schoolboy, schoolgirl, undergraduate, apprentice, and on-job learner. Nevertheless, the complexity of being a student is beyond the initial explanation of student having identity of uniforms, classrooms, having teachers at the front or school bags with notebooks. Studentship is related to continuous learning at different stages of life. We learn from cradle to grave. Anyone who stops learning is about to die. Studentship is core area of life that sustains humanity. We discover. We die. Yet we live on. Why? Because somebody has to bend so low under a tutor to learn before he/she (tutor) dies with the knowledge and this is called knowledge transfer. Therefore, everyone on the earth surface is a prospective and potential student. This book is applicable to you as long as you aspire to learn and learn, in order to solve problems you met and the one you created. We live in the society that everyone wants to teach without gaining more knowledge. A university graduate may believe that all needed requirements for fulfilment have been given within the space of four to five years. And therefore, he/she may not want to learn as a student again. Knowledge grows as we grow. Knowledge is attached to change occurrences. What we knew ten years ago is archaic to this present age. Even what you know today will become obsolete in ten years' time. If you refuse to learn more, you will be obsolete too in ten years' time.

We must learn to live together as brothers or perish together as fools – Martin Luther King Jr.

Education is what remains after one has forgotten one has learned in school – Albert Einstein

Student has composition of internal and external structures which establish atmosphere for learning, practicing, creating, discovering, and researching for more. The major and active organ that keeps a student going is the mind. Going to formal school like primary, secondary and tertiary institution may not totally qualify a student as one who learns until he/she has the main tool and ingredient of studentship which is the mind. Everyone has mind, yet the mind of student is different. Norman Vincent Peale,[ii] the writer of *You Can If You Think You Can,* narrates a story of his professor, Mr. Reeves. This professor appeared in the classroom and one day he wrote on the board the word "CAN'T". Turning to the class and said, "Knock the T off the CAN'T." Student gazed at him. The prof. erased the T, leaving the word "CAN" standing out clear and strong. He said, "Let that be a lesson to you. You are meant to grow up into strong, competent people believing in yourselves, in your country and in God. You are not designed to be little weak pygmies. You are to develop into real men and women and, I'm telling you that you can make something of yourselves. And to do that, never forget this principle of success: *'you can if you think you can.'*" This proves that all students have minds to think and change their world. If starts from the belief that you can.

Learning without thought is labour lost – Confucius

This mind of student is filled with different options, views, aspirations, worldviews and possibilities. The strength of being a student resides in the mind. When a student loses his/her mind, all means to learn is gone. The heroes of great discovery discovered the power of their mind and they began to think, sustain the thought and improve the idea for human consumptions. The mind of student has multitudes of things such as desires for success, passions to get all marks, dreams of tomorrow, career options and development, quick progress, possibility of all things, seeing full support and approval of all that he/she thinks, believes all his/her attempt as correct, and the power to freely create without barrier. Discouragement is just letters without effect in the mind of student who determines to learn. It is the Mind who connects the whole system of student to the teacher, class activities and doing the learning. If the mind is discouraged, there will be loss of interest in learning class, teacher and the career; it may also lead to failure; truancy; disturbance; loss of appetite for reading, addiction, peer pressure involvement, etc.

Your mind will answer most questions if you learn to relax and wait for the answer – William S. Burroughs

Mind is an internal structure that cannot be seen but has power of making things happen. Mind is the sole mental activities of a person and also memory-stick for student. The mind includes both conscious thoughts and unconscious activity such as dreaming. The human identity can be viewed as being made of mind and body. Many philosophies and religions also recognize another aspect of identity, the soul.[iii] Almost everyone is adherent to one religion and the other. We believe the human composition has mind to think, evaluate, judge, criticize, create, make, propose and imagine anything before action takes place. It is the blessing of God to man. As a student, you are well equipped to learn, view, imagine and act whatever you are taught because your body structure is wonderfully and fearfully made.[iv] Mind is abstract but its effect is observable. Mind is the functionality of the brain. Every student has brain. Active brain makes you active student.

If brain has impact on learning, then what is brain? Brain[v] is a portion of the central nervous system contained within the skull.

The brain is the control center for movement, sleep, hunger, thirst, and virtually every other vital activity necessary to survival. All human emotions—including love, hate, fear, anger, elation, and sadness—are controlled by the brain. It also receives and interprets the countless signals that are sent to it from other parts of the body and from the external environment. The brain makes us conscious, emotional, and intelligent. Learning and behavioural actions take place in the brain. Walter Mischel[vi] in late in the 20th century wrote that methods for observing the activity of the living brain were developed that made it possible to explore links between what the brain is doing and psychological phenomena, thus opening a window into the relationship between the mind, brain, and behaviour.[vii] Georges Rey[viii] posed a question, "Could a computer have a mind? What would it take to create a computer that could have a specific thought, emotion, or experience?" Perhaps a computer could have a mind only if it were made up of the same kinds of neurons and chemicals of which human brains are composed.[ix] Which means mind of students have what computer does not have. This is magnificent work of God. When a person has head-injury, he/she has tendency of losing thought of past events and his/her speech may not tally with others because the brain (the mind) is injured. A sick student may not be able to learn. In this book, I will deal with problems that affect student's mind such as health negligence, etc.

Live as if you were to die tomorrow. Learn as if you were to live forever – Mahatma Gandhi

Mind of the student is intertwined with target; success at all cost. Student without success is like a bird that lays eggs without hatching them. Success is from within. If you cannot imagine it before the lesson, term, semester or session starts, you may not be able to get it right. This issue will be discussed elaborately in this book. Every student has potential problems related to mind and these problems have hindered many for donkey years from achieving their set goals within the years of schooling. Some of these problems are curiosity, laziness, distraction, wrong decisions, procrastination, reading sickness, religiosity, inferiority, etc. All these problems will be carefully deciphered in this book. Also, the mind of student has power to create, solve, make and make better. Every successful hero believes in their mind objectivity that they could create something new that will solve the problems they met and the one they created in the process of living. You can formulate theories, formula, principles and laws. You can use your brain to solve societal challenges through your profession. In this book, I will keep challenging you to be the first in Africa to discover anti-Ebola vaccine, anti-corruption formula, sixth sense technology,[x] solar energy in the dark, new mathematical theory after your name, new device and system for electricity power supply, anti-cyber detector without internet, creation of new vocabularies, think-tank of the nation policy formulation, etc. Strength generated from your vibrant brain and healthy mind cannot be underemphasized. It is really on your side now. You have opportunity to think wide, store up information, criticize constructively, review and diagnose issues, decide and judge with your potential cerebrums. Your mind is healthy enough to imagine length and breadth of nature. You can achieve your dream as long as you see yourself as a student that keeps learning. Think right. Your mind has the capacity. A research shows that only few percentage of the brain (mind) is used by a genius[xi] when new thing is discovered. The geniuses used to work creatively to explore more ideas like wright brothers[xii] in aviation development.[xiii] And till now what have you discovered?

Education is the most powerful weapon which you can use to change the world – Nelson Mandela

In this book, I will guide you to see different worlds of students you may belong and how to achieve your dream within the space. Also, the way to examination breakthrough shall be examined. However, the age of studentship has difficulties that must be managed. Studentship has no regard for age. A twenty (20) years old boy with seventy (70) years old man shall be treated equally in the classroom because learning is impartial. If you are aged without student's mind, you cannot learn. A youth that is agile for learning with student's mind and unable to deal with distractions warring for mind will equally face the same challenge with a person without mind for learning. These distractions are: sexual immorality, moral decadence, music madness, media tricks, fashion trend, pride, unguided politics, cultism, peer pressure, unguided exposure, etc. All these will be treated in this book for better learning. If you eventually prosper as a student, you still must watch out for enemies of progress that war within you; though you suffer and smile. They are called depression of the mind. This book exposes you to the management of depression as a student with learning mind. Other topics treated are limitations to the mind of students and the place of God in achieving your goals with a learning mind for He is the author and guide to all minds. God knows your thought before it comes out into action. Therefore, this book will address your relationship with God for excellence.

Mind of student is the thing that everyone needs to possess to change oneself, environment, labour market, culture, suffering level, choice, beliefs, value system and actions. Norman Vincent Peale, also the author of *The Power of Positive Thinking*,[xiv] notes that all resources you need are in your mind. God made man complete with a sound mind that thinks productively. He breathed in man, power of creation like Him. Man can make anything from what God created as raw materials. All inventions are from the mind. It means the chair you are sitting on was in somebody's mind many years ago. Mind of students from past decades produced vehicle, washing machine, phones, television, drugs, vaccine, cooking process, books, clothes, camera, etc. If you do not explore your mind, you will just become an ordinary keeper of many other great gadgets that would have made life easier for others. A motivational and seasoned teacher of the Word, Sam Adeyemi[xv] says "Ideas rule the world". But I say that the idea that remains inactive in the mind will only rule the abstract world of the conceiver. You must give birth to your ideas when other people are yet to conceive and deliver theirs; for ideas can be obsolete if it is not unveiled at the right time.

The aim of education should be to teach us how to think, rather than what to think. To improve our minds, so as to enable us to think for ourselves, rather than to load the memory with other men – Bill Beattice

I've learned... that the best classroom in the world is at the feet of an elderly person – Andy Rooney

In the mind, there is space for knowledge accumulation. Knowledge is known as information; it is formed by the numbers of data you get from reliable sources, classrooms, online, books, outdoor, tutors, experiences, etc. In this book, you will get knowledge. Knowledge can save forty (40) years of your life from stress and struggle with four (4) hours of privilege information. Your mind cannot operate in vacuum. It needs information that will translate into knowledge. No one is born with knowledge. We live to learn and store up. Every mind has plain tablet that we inscribe on daily basis. Wrong information will make a wrong mind to give wrong knowledge that will consume the human race in war, insurgence, kidnapping, etc. When you ruminate on the right knowledge, it becomes understanding that can solve related problems. Knowledge can be sourced through learning. Mind is always set to learn if the host has access to knowledge. Mind is like a new vehicle who wants to roll on the street of the city but there is no fuel and driver. If a wrong driver sits to drive, the vehicle will have accident. Also if you have right driver without fuel, the vehicle will not move. Having the right information and translation into knowledge through constant and consistent learning will drive on the mind of the student to success.

Education is not preparation for life. Education is life itself – John Dewey

There are seven (7) ways of learning. You can learn through:[xvi] observation, interrogation, research, apprenticeship, participation, meditation, and reading. **Observation**: When you keenly and purposefully watch a thing without questioning or participating; therefore, observation has occurred. The mind of student works fast when it sees a new thing with keen interest to know more. Observation injects curiosity into the mind of student to take more steps into the reason for what is observed. Learning through observation can be used in the classroom during practical session, lecture, exposition or when an incident occurs with amazement to everyone. You will not just watch to please your eyes alone but to feed your mind with possibility of stopping such occurrence in the nearest future.

The beautiful thing about learning is that no one can take it away from you – B. B. King

Interrogation/Questioning:

When you are inquisitive about something in form of questioning, then interrogation is in process. The student with mind of learning will not watch alone. If he/she has opportunity to ask question, he/she will go ahead before others. It is a pity today in our schools that only few students ask questions during learning time. I discovered that a student who asks questions is always ahead of others. Questioning is a skill of the mind. You have seen a picture which is not really clear and to get it right, you ask questions that will cause the teacher to speak more on the subjects. Shyness and incompetence of some students deny them complete knowledge. Anyone who has mind to learn will plan before the class begins with questions that will clarify the learning of the day. Not only in the classroom, students with mind of learning can interrogate anyone, no matter the status; just to feed their mind with correct update for learning. A student should not always accept all things; hook and sinker. Questioning can be in form of probing, querying, examining and inquiries on why, how, what and when of a subject matter. Ask questions from parents, lecturers, teachers, friends, acquaintance, professionals and anyone who has the knowledge of what you need for learning. There is no harm in questioning. However, you must be constructive and intelligent in your approach as you question anyone, for respect is reciprocal.

I never learn anything talking. I only learn things when I ask questions – Lon Holtz

Research:

This is a bit close to interrogation but farther in term, time and results. Research for information may last many years, just to formulate data to solve problems. The researcher will go extra mile to expose what, where, why and how of a thing. I wonder why our tertiary instructions in Africa are not proffering solutions to our problems. A student's mind should always aspire to develop solution. Research starts from the mind. The picture you see will prompt you to go on. Research has challenges that can halt the process, but a mind that wants to solve problems will not stop. Solution to our problems is not far from us. Only the mind of student can see it. When last do you think about what you use daily and how you can reduce the cost through your invention? Africa is a dumping ground for other continental products. We buy, use and trash after use. We cannot even manage our waste. Other advanced countries do research, discover, produce, sell, use and recycle their trash for another products. I wish my reader will have mind for invention through research work. You can start with what is available around you. Learning through trial by error ends with great invention. Just believe in yourself that you can do it.

You don't learn to walk by following rules. You learn by doing, and by falling over – Richard Branson

What we learn to do, we learn by doing – Thomas Jefferson

Apprenticeship:

It is the act of bending or bowing low to learn under a person for a duration agreed by the parties. A student's mind has sincere humility to learn from anyone despite the age difference, status difference or intelligent variance. In a class, there is always intelligent variance; all fingers are not equal. If you don't mind, you can derive your intelligence from others who know the subjects better. It is a matter of time. A shared knowledge encourages learning. Schooling without practical knowledge of a course is a cheat of years spent in the four walls of institutions. Many graduates today cannot operate, analyze, prove, or practice what they studied.[xvii] Education without practicality is like an electronic gadget without power supply; it will lie idle and useless. Anyone who wants to learn will strengthen his/her mind to see others as blessing in disguise. You can be an apprentice at home, in the school under a teacher, or in an innovation school under an instructor. Africa peculiarity and beauty is looking up to students with extra skills above academic gymnastics; who is entrepreneur in nature. What you don't know, you don't know. And what you bend to know will become part of you; it is a matter of your mind.

Tell me and I forget. Teach me and I remember. Involve me and I Learn – Benjamin Franklin

Participation:

When there is collective effort in discovering data with the expert. The novice will be allowed to do the miniature work while watching the professional doing the core ones. Team spirit survives when student's mind for learning is in operation. Participation breeds collective results. When you want to do it alone, you may not get it all. Those people who invented some gadgets did not monopolize knowledge, they shared responsibility in teamwork. A student who desires results will discover a truth, share with like-minded people and through brainstorming, a result that will solve problems will be discovered. An example is Wright Brothers[xviii] who invented Airplane together through participation.

Meditation:

The act of ruminating on what has been observed, questioned, researched, participated and read in calm and solitude mood. Sam Adeyemi in his book *Multiply Your Success Lead,*[xix] also adds that meditation is the art of dreaming. Dream comes from the mind. Mind itself has power to generate solution within. No mind works in isolation. What you feed your mind is what it shall meditate over. The principle of regurgitation[xx] in ruminant animals can help in learning through mediation. Whenever a sheep finds a pasture, she will be happy to eat as much as she can. She will swallow grasses with little chewing. After a moment of ups and downs, she will find a conducive environment to regurgitate. She will bring back the food, bit by bit, into her mouth for rigorous chewing and digestion. A student's mind needs raw data to mediate upon. There is need to observe quietness for thinking over the data. I learnt that most inventors spent hours in their study rooms to look over, study, think, and mediate on possibilities and later try the outcomes. As a student who wants to solve problems, you need a study room where you analyze your thought over the day. Your study room may be an open air space with quietness, in a park, a garden, library, or waiting room. Meditation goes with act of jotting/writing. When you mediate, you must pen down your thought in black and white for our memory is not a computer that keeps many files. You express your mind on paper. According to Brian Tracy, writer of *Eat That Frog*[xxi] asserts that only 3 percent of adults have clear, written goals. All think but never write down their goals. When you meditate, you organize your thought on priority. What you write is a fuel in the furnace of achievement. The more you read, think, and think over your write up, the greater it becomes your inner drive and desire to accomplish them.

Reading:

This is an act of gleaning data and information from written books. When you sit back to read from books, you sit to learn from those who are dead or alive, far or near, in a solitude and readiness to change, you learn more. Learning by reading should be at least one hour every day. Reading is easy and simple if you possess mind of student. I remembered when I was in the seminary, reading of books was a rigorous exercise because the mind of *"I cannot do it"* was in me and it limited my approach. Until when I began to love and glean new facts, then I fell in love with reading, not just for examination purpose but for personal consumption. Reading books in schools today is 10% below average. Though some schools' library do not have current and relevant books, yet a student with mind for learning will find opportunity of getting the needed and useful books. I read a national newspaper[xxii] and I was marveled with a story of lady who graduated with first class. She narrated her ordeal that her younger sister had to drop out from school for her to get tuition paid. With this plight, she was unable to buy books related to her courses. She said, *"I go online to search for free books and print them"*. Today, she is a scholar and lecturer in the school. Reading makes you a relevant person and educated elite.

There is no end to education. It is not that read a book, pass an examination, and finish with education. The whole life, from moment you are born to the moment you die, is a process of learning – Jiddu Krishnamurti

Who is an educated person? He is a person who knows something about everything and everything about something. Reading qualifies you for that. Mind of student should be filled with understanding of core information of your field and various issues that are not closely related to your field of learning. This makes you a relevant person. Reading a book brings the author closer to you. You are in the mind of the author when he/she wrote the book. Reading transfers mind-to-mind knowledge.

Reading with exposure strengthens mind of student. Sam Adeyemi[xxiii] notes that reading makes a whole world of difference. He shared his experience he got from books he read after graduation. He caught a vision of a large church, though a jobless graduate. He said and I quote, *"God's Spirit took what I read and burned some pictures in my heart. My heart was hot as I was reading those books, listening to tapes and watching videos. Exposure matters"*.

The more you learn, the more you can learn. A professor will die but his professional works still impacting after him, while an illiterate man will reduce to ashes of nothingness. He cannot add any value to his world and such person lives on suggested influence of others in the society because he cannot contribute but consume. Just as you can build your physical muscles through physical exercises, so also you can build your brain, mental muscles with mental exercises through a learning mind. There is no limit to how far or how fast you can advance except for the limits you place on your own imaginations. The Bible even says, "I can do everything through him who gives me strength."[xxiv] You have the capacity to learn and solve problems if you possess mind of student.

Do you know Wilfredo Pareto, the Italian economist? He coined a principle called "Pareto Principle"[xxv] – 20% vital few and 80% trivial many. It is a management skill used to manage human resources based on priority. This principle can be applied to mind of student. It is not all information you get that must sink down into the mind as student. You need to sieve for the relevance. Also your effort as young person now will account for your achievement at the latter end of life. The more you learn now, the more you enjoy buoyant resources within you. A scholar does 20% of rigorous learning to achieve 80% returns. As a young student with fertile, fresh and proactive mind, 20% of your learning activities – educative learning or acquiring skill – will account for 80% of your results. Your schooling effort at teen and youthful age will determine your lifetime remuneration, career success and old age survival. If you are to live 80 years, 20% of your life is 16 years and if 100 years it is 20 years. Whatever you are able to acquire within age range of 15 years to 40 years of your life will equal to delicacies on your table, comfortable shelter for your body, contribution to the society, service to God and benefit for old age. Most inventors got breakthrough of their inventions when they were at their prime age. Exercise your mind for learning when all strength to think is still on your side. Most of our parents do not achieve their aims for life due to unexpected intrusions into their schooling. When you become a parent, you achieve little because of welfare provision for the family. The time of studentship is short. Meaningful things can still be done. Orison Swett Marden[xxvi] says and I quote that, "Every great man has become great, every successful man has succeeded in proportion as he has confined his powers to one particular channel." Jack of all trade will never achieve anything. Doing 'this' and doing 'that' only sap strength to achieve zero. If you are a student, face your studies now. Let your mind be settled and focused on learning. Disallow distractions of this age. The world at a large is waiting for your input that will solve the problems you met and the one you created. The mind of student is a learning mind. Desire it.

CHAPTER TWO

TARGET IN THE MIND OF STUDENT

According to Mike Murdock[xxvii], in his book *The Assignment*, the matter of purpose is analyzed based on assignment. Did you know that God created you to solve problems? Why do you have a bag? Because it solved books conveyance problems. Why do you watch news each evening on television? It solves an information problem. God create your mind to solve your problems and community problems. As a student, you go to school to solve literacy problem. If you shall solve the problem, you must have some targets in your mind as propeller for your flight. Target can be object aimed at in shooting especially at archery, rifle shooting, and similar sports. It can be when somebody or something aimed at an area, surface, object, or person.[xxviii] For this book, target is a goal - a goal or objective toward which effort is directed. Mind of student survives on goal. Mind can be crowded if there is no law of priority and goal settings. Everything that glitters usually appeals to the eyes and minds. We want all things but we cannot have all things. You must have a target for life. In career development, some students find it difficult to choose a career for future because all professions appeal to their mind. Such student needs to develop interest with a target on one course. Interest level for a course must go beyond likeness. No profession exists without challenges. To be a trained doctor, you must develop strong affinity for patients at any state of life. There will be a time when failures and mistakes come up; you cannot because of that quit the profession. Target for student grows as you learn. Every target has consequences. Brain Tracy says,[xxix] "The mark of the superior thinker is his/her ability to accurately predict the consequences of doing or not doing something".

Target has to do with long term process. It is a picture seen by the conceiver and will be nursed for fulfilment after many years of perspiration and inspiration. Students want to excel academically. This is the hallmark of studentship that he/she has success after the learning. Success is not cheap. Success is scarce but available for mind of student who keeps learning. Success is not on the surface; it is hidden for the serious minded students. Precious things are not exposed. You dig and dig to explore. Gold, diamond, costly stones, crude oil, etc. are not on the surface for lazy exploiters. Success is not for a lazy student. It is good to have a target and it is also better to work towards the target.

Target can be dreams of tomorrow. Many dreams have failed and faded away from the mind of the conceivers because the dream lacks strength to survive long term process. Many chose career because of parent pressure, influence or peer pressure. Such target will fail. Some parents even set target with bias motive such as dignity and prestige a particular career has in the society; family dynasty of a career; shame and penury attached to some careers; illiterate and ignorance; their friends' children also choose the career; the future risk and threat on job security; wrong advice; the joy of having a child at the stage of choosing career; less information about career; spiritual intonation and divinity; traces and traits/skill they discovered when the child was a kid; and singleness and divorce pain. All these will strangle success in the mind of the student.

No success without pain. Students that will have success will burn night candle of reading and learning to get ever bright future without nightlight. What do you see in your future? Do you have purpose for your reading? Future intent influences and often determines present actions. Successful students are those who are willing to delay gratification and sacrifices in the short term so that they can enjoy greater rewards in the long term. The unsuccessful students, on the other hand, think more about short term pleasure and immediate enjoyment while giving little thought to the long term future. Do not assume bigness as long as you are a student for now; diligently grow in hardworking, learning, apprenticeship, studying and researching from the "Big Ones" – I mean your teachers, parents, lecturers, senior ones, boss, and instructors without counting the pain, shame, humiliation and denials. They are short time sacrifices for big time and lasting enjoyment. Your target will encourage you.

Target of the student is absolute success. Success speaks louder than words. It commands greater attention than the greatest oration any man can make. It is self-inviting and attractive. Success has a compelling force around it, drawing everyone to itself, whether consciously or unconsciously. Success has different views according to individuals' definitions. Success is achievement of intention: the achievement of something planned or attempted. When something turns out well as planned or intended. However, some call it accumulation of wealth, building big houses, winning political campaign, traveling over the sea every day, having the stocks of shares, etc. As student, it may be just to pass examinations with better grades, having awards and prize, winning scholarship, etc. However, all these are good but for me, success is the ability to discover a problem and proffer solution that will outlive the provider. African are prosperous people with all human resources but with wrong definition of success. They acquire wealth for other continent to use. They corrupt the Africa system of governance because their target is wrong. A student with right mind will study to solve problems. We need right leaders with sincere target and commitment to humanity. Can we count on you as one who will solve Africa's problem? It is the matter of your mind. Corruption starts from the mind. Determine to stay away from it and save our continent. Mind of the student needs to understand the law behind success. Success is not for all. For every proactive step to success, a law must be understood and obeyed. Let's consider the laws of success that are applicable to students.

Laws of Success

The first law of success is concentration.
It is when the mind of student has a focus at one direction with effort towards one particular task, idea, or subject at a time. It

involves bending all the energies to one point, and to go directly to that point, looking neither to the right nor to the left. The Bible also has clue to this point. This was the law that God gave to Joshua after Moses death, *"Be strong and courageous, because you will lead these people to inherit the land I swore to their forefathers to give them. Be strong and very courageous. Be careful to obey all the law my servant Moses gave you; do not turn from it to the right or to the left, that you may be successful wherever you go."*[xxx] Paul also obeyed the law – "I do not consider myself yet to have taken hold of it. But one thing I do: Forgetting what is behind and straining toward what is ahead, I press on toward the goal to win the prize for which God has called me heavenward in Christ Jesus."[xxxi] Pressing, straining, and focusing on one thing enhances concentration that distraction cannot withstand. Law of success has just one goal to achieve. Vincent Norman Peale states that,[xxxii] the goal must not be vague or fuzzy but a sharply focused objective. You must know what you want to do and where you want to go, what you want to be. And have no doubt about it. The next step is to pray about the one goal to be sure it is a right objective, because if it is not right, it's wrong and nothing wrong ever works right. What to do to concentrate on your goal: Do things that are very important, something that you must do – like reading and studying. Delegate what others can do for you. Delete what you know are not necessary for your life and delay what is important but not urgent till another day. Student who lacks concentration will not achieve success. You must plan your thought over everything you want. You cannot be a journalist and still be a doctor at the same time. You cannot read Biology and still solve Mathematics together. One thing at a time.

You need to concentrate on what you believe you can do - your passion, skill, talent and inspiration. Do not allow discouragement to slip off your vision. Remind your mind everyday 'I will make it'. It will become a miracle like Walt Disney. This is the miracle story of a young artist who believed in himself though he was very poor.[xxxiii] The story begins long ago in Kansas

City. A young fellow with an urge to draw went from newspaper to newspaper trying to sell his cartoons. But each editor coldly, and perhaps a bit cruelly, informed him that he had no talent and advised him to forget it. But he couldn't forget the dream, for it had grabbed him and would not let go. The dream lived in his mind.   How can you forget a powerful motivation? Finally a pastor employed the young man at a pittance (subsistence wage) to draw advertising pictures for church events. But the fledging artist had to have a "studio," another way of describing a place to sleep as well as to draw. It seems the church had an old mouse-infested garage and he was told he could stay there. One of those mice he used to see daily in the garage became world-famous, as did the young artist. The mouse became known to millions as Mickey Mouse; the artist was Walt Disney. When I read this story my concentration increased on what I know best. I refused to give up to discouragement of poverty and rejection. The law of success will prevail if you do not quit. How do you keep your mind on the goal? The answer is: Keep thinking, keep the interest, keep praying, and keep dreaming. Be mentally sensitive at all times to every opportunity for development and improvement. It may be now. How ready are you?

The second law of success is sincere self-grading.

Give yourself a grade. Isaiah once did it, *""Woe to me!" I cried. "I am ruined! For I am a man of unclean lips..."*[xxxiv] You know your strength and weakness better than anyone does. Your strength preserves time while weakness consumes time. Use all available opportunities to identify your weakness to improve on it positively. You can analyze your worth with SWOT – Strength, Weakness, Opportunity and Threat Analysis. Your mind is the best evaluator of your worth. If others deceive you, I know you will not deceive yourself. Self-grading will guide you on your journey to success. What you are aiming to do, can you do it? Are you prepared to embark on the race? Can you study that course? Here is another relevant question you will ever ask and answer. *"What one skill will have the greatest positive impact in my life and career, if I develop and do it in an excellent way?"* As from now and henceforth, do what you can, and what you should with what you have where you are.

The third law of success is immediate action.

Learn to take immediate action that will transform your life, for procrastination steals time and opportunities. Procrastination[xxxv] is called deferment, postponement, stalling, delay, putting off, adjournment, and suspension. Whatever you mind prompt you to do, write it down. Do research on it without delay. It may the solution you are waiting for. In colleges, teachers instruct you for immediate action but in tertiary institutions, it depends on you alone - no close and persuasive instructors. Assignment will be given without thinking about your convenience or schedule for domestic works. Start to do right things at the right time with immediate effort. Success calls for single step action. A journey of a thousand miles begins with a single step. Therefore, no matter the level of your ability, you have more potential than you can ever develop in a lifetime.

The fourth law of success is learning.

You aim higher to be great in your career and life, and then learn what you need to learn so that you can be what you dream of. For continuous learning is the minimum requirement for success in any field. (You can refer back to chapter one to read more).

Success has some other ingredients for potential student. They are: determination, planning, decision, deadlines and evaluation.

Determination

The root of determination comes from the mind. Some determined minds say, "I will succeed", "I will get it right", "I can do it", "With God, it is possible", etc. Being optimistic about your studies is the final work of your mind. You don't look at the gigantic structure of problem; you see the simple techniques to solve the problem. It all comes from determination. If you give a student who has determined to fail all answers to examinations, he/she will still fail. That is the will power of man. Going to school is determination that goes beyond parental influence, likeness of school structure or friendship in the school. It involves your life and purpose. If you miss it, you may not get it back in time. Success begins her journey with determination. Do you believe in success through malpractices? If yes, then you cannot read to pass. Unless you change your mind, malpractice will always appeal to your senses. Determination gives birth to your planning.

Planning

Planning flows from the mind of student who has determined to move on with a vision. A vision is essentially a picture of the destination in mind or on paper. It is a journey from where you are to where you want to be. However, you will still need to develop a systematic plan for its accomplishment. Adequate planning flows from a determined mind. There is a warning. Before you begin climbing up the ladder of success, make sure the ladder is leaning against the right building to avoid sudden fall.[xxxvi] I have these instructions for you. One of the very worst uses of time, I mean lifetime, is to do something very well that need not to be done at all. This is purely abuse of lifetime. The days used for wrong assignment cannot be regained even after doing the right. And taking actions without thinking through is a prime source of these pitfalls. To avoid these pitfalls, planning is incontrovertible and indispensable, i.e. planning of your strength within the days when mind is potent. Planning is bringing the future into the present so that you can do something about it now. Your future starts now. The strength you have has already started countdown. Mind of student does not wait for anyone to stir up for reading. He/she knows when to read, study and practice. Effort of a determined mind moves to planning that will translate to wise decision.

Decision

This is evident in action. Anyone who sees your actions may predict your mind. Some psychologists use human behaviour which is the product of one's decision as the measure to know the person in and out. Wrong decision is bad and indecision is evil. Some decisions may not be corrected due to the havoc it must have caused the person, community and the nations. Sam

Adeyemi[xxxvii] notes the fragility of decision. He posed some questions. "Before you jump from your present course, school, job or career, please ask yourself a few questions. Why do you want to move? Why do you want to abandon your vision, school, class or career? Why are you going to abandon the invention? Hold on! Are you assuming that there is perfect school, job, work, course, relationship or project? Is it simply you want to escape some hardship? Some hardship and suffering may be part of your training. You need positive attitude that flows from a mind that wants to learn". Mind of student should test, measure and count worth of decisions before taking them. However, every decision calls for immediate follow up, for society has power to kill, manipulate or mar it. Think twice before you make a choice in life. Your decision today will be your praise or regret tomorrow. Be careful in choosing marital partner, friends, job, course, project and a career especially as a secondary school leaver. For anyone who wants to make a choice for life (career), kindly answers these questions.[xxxviii]

1. What do you want to become in life?
2. What do you want to spend the active days of life on?
3. What can you do to change and make history in my generation?
4. What are you created to solve?
5. Why do you want to choose this career?
6. Are you on pressure or peer group influence?
7. Do you have capacity for this career?
8. Does your personality go with this career?
9. Does your academic performance have capacity for this career?
10. What are your strengths for this career?
11. What are your weaknesses against this career?
12. Are there any threats that can abort the process of achieving this career?
13. Are there visible or intangible opportunities awaiting me after the training for this career?
14. What is your endurance level to education?

15.   Does the career appeal to your parents' support?

16.   Is there any good citadel of learning that offers the course of study around you?

17.   Can you disregard irrelevant options for this career?

18.   Will you be able to accept the good, the bad and the ugly of this career?

19.   Will you be able to encourage others to choose this career after many years of practice?

20.   How pleasing is your choice to God?

21.   Do you go to school with strong passion to learn?

22.   Do you have favourite subjects?

23.   Do you have ugliest subjects and why?

24.   Do you have interest in your subjects' teachers?

25.   Do you see beyond classroom at the time you learn under your teacher?

26.   Do you teach others some subjects?

27.   Do you score above average in some subjects?

28.   How many hours do you spend per day on reading?

29.   Does your assimilation last for months or days on each subject?

30.   Do you struggle to pick point when you read alone or you love general reading?

31.   Are you habitual in reading?

32.   Do you have time for co-curricular readings?

33.   How often do you visit library for research?

34.   Do you experiment what you learn daily from the classroom?

35.   Do you have access to quality and essential books for studying?

36.   How effective and smart are you on time management when you read to do exam?

37.   Do you interact with what you learn when you get home with your friends, families and colleagues?

38.   Can you memorize formula, principles, theories, and procedures for long?

39. Do you have a working method of assimilation and remembering formula, principles, theories, and procedures?
40. Do you see your career development as you read?
41. Here is another acid test for your personality structure for successful career.
42. Do you like or love yourself?
43. Are you pleased whenever people talk about your excesses and shortcomings?
44. Do you think before you talk or talk before you think?
45. Do you love to relate with people at first sight?
46. How social you are to friends and strangers?
47. Do you love to calculate all things for accuracy?
48. Do you prefer to stay alone and do things?
49. Do you loss heart when you are intimidated or accused?
50. Are you keen about new things?
51. Do you bother about creatures and their survival?
52. Do you feel emotional pain when someone feels hurt?
53. Do you ask questions to establish facts or just to keep company busy?
54. Do you see creativity on everything you see or can imagine?
55. Are you lousy or reserved?
56. Do you always find a way to express yourself when others do not?
57. Do you know what you can do best?
58. Have you scrutinized yourself (personality) with the dream career?
59. Do you see where your strength can fit in in any career?
60. How will you adjust, improve or deliberately nurture some features that can sustain your career?
61. Where is the school located?
62. What are the attractive things that lure you to this school?
63. What are the amenities she has for learning?

64. How affordable is the school in monetary term?
65. Does the school have unbroken years of study without labour strike? If not, why?
66. What is the economic life in the school?
67. Does the school have successful product in the career I want?
68. Does the school uphold discipline and security of lives of students?
69. Does the school environment grow good citizens of Nigeria or cultists?
70. Does the society accept the certificate of this school in practice of my dream career?
71. Is the school faith-based, government-owned or private?
72. Is there any international affiliation with the dream career through the school?
73. Is the school appealing to my parents/guardians?
74. Will my parents/guardians accept the school terms and policy on training?

Deadlines

One of the best ways for students to overcome procrastination is by working as though you had only one day to get your most important work done. When you discover a truth/fact, do not delay to know more. Whenever an assignment is given, you do not wait till teacher begins to place pressure on you. Place pressure on yourself by burning your night candle now. Put pressure on yourself now before third parties such as society, parents, families, religion, friends, marriage, and age put pressure on you. Create imaginary deadlines for yourself and strive hard to achieve them before age and time of studentship knocks you down. Youthful age has deadlines. Passion to be (exuberance) and drive to imagine (intuition) is for a while. Whatever you achieve with them is what will be in your archives for life. What you do is what you have done. No one will add to it. Use the opportunity of life to achieve your schooling. Opportunity is neither friend nor foe. Opportunity comes down like simple and gentle bubbles which will later grow wild with soaring wings like eagle and it disappears into the thin air of no return. Opportunity of parents; I mean, good, reliable and responsible parents, opportunity of good education, opportunity of good learning materials, opportunity of sound mind and good health are not forever. Opportunity comes with distractions and fallacy. Opportunity has enemy – called distractions. Technology is your friend but can also be a distractor if not managed. Addiction to food, lust, romantic novels, music, fashion, friendship, sporting, betting, partying and so on can speedily become catalyst hormones that will develop wings for your opportunities to fly away (it shall be discussed in chapter eight). Life and opportunity are not permanent friends. Opportunity of life comes in mask and does not look attractive. Consequently, many have ignored its lovely appealing. A lost opportunity is lost forever – bitter truth. The consequences are future regret, horror and pain of waiting for another opportunities, shame and contempt in the neighbourhood. Whenever another opportunity surfaces, there will be no more equal strength, support, structure, satisfaction, and interest to use as they were. Use the deadline strategy for success as a student with learning mind.

Intelligence is not to make no mistakes, but quickly to see how to make them good – Bertolt Brecht

Evaluation

Success is a journey. The sojourner needs compass to check regularly if he/she is on the track. When a person determines to go to success arena and the planning is superb. There is need to constantly put yourself to test to know how far and how well you are doing. Most students read and study while attempting any question. It is like filling a drum without knowing the capacity of the container. If the drum is bent, or having hole, all the effort will be wasted. Periodically, check your seriousness with your target. The goal at the end should be compared with the present achievement. If they are commensurate to one another, success is sure. Sometimes, we see failure, when we periodically check ourselves. Failure is not a disease. It is a test on your capacity, endurance and tolerance. A lecturer once told me a life principle that says,[xxxix] "Whenever you make progress in what you know best, do not laugh but smile. Whenever you fail despite your effort, do not cry but be frank. Sit down and research why you progress so that you can monitor and master the pace. Your failure also needs investigation to know the weak point to strengthen. What others do and fail. You can do it and be successful". Do not compare yourself to lose taste of your uniqueness. Mind of student has good sense of progress at all level of life.

Anyone who has never made a mistake has never tried anything new – Albert Einstein

Success is possible for student who determines to plan based on decision that has deadlines garnished with periodic evaluation exercise. All come from mind that is ready to learn.

CHAPTER THREE

PROBLEMS ASSOCIATED WITH THE MIND OF STUDENT

*I am not afraid of storms for I am learning how to sail my ship –
Louisa May Alcott*

Anything that provides comfort and solution to others can also have problem if it is not managed well. Mind of student serves the student in learning, yet it has some associate problems that may reduce its effectiveness on the long run. Precaution is better than cure is the proactive way of managing mind of student who wants to learn. Since the mind is a vast reservoir of needed resources, any kind of foreign issues may block off the orderliness of thought and hinder right thinking. These obstacles can be self-imposed and externally imputed. Vincent Norman Peale says,[xl] "Everything goes wrong because I'm wrong". Mind is flexible to wrong things. Students have access to people, places, books, lifestyles, movies, ideas, etc. that can make or mar their mind. Have you seen a boy who has a promising future in medicine, and suddenly has a change of mind to join bad boys in the campus and latter leads him to addiction and truancy? There is wrong influence on his mind. Influence has great effects on student's mind that does not guard against such. Campus is a big world with a mixture of visionless, carefree and no-future-ambition students. Even in secondary schools, students that love pleasure and fun will exchange their future fast for fun. May you not become the victim.

We shall examine some highlighted problems that can likely affect the mind of students in tertiary institutions, at home and other citadel.

Problem one – Curiosity
Curiosity is common to human beings at all ages from infancy through adulthood, and is easy to observe in many other animal

species. These include apes, cats, and rodents. Everyone has curiosity but the level defers. Without curiosity, we will not be able to learn. However, it can still be misused. As a student, learning is sustained by the level of curiosity of a student. We see a doctor in the hospital and we sometimes want to touch the stethoscope because we want to know it through sense of touch. Our parents fight us because we do not take permission before we operate, press or handle a gadget in the house. If you are curious to be a lawyer, it is good if it leads you to read, study and get prepared systematically but if it leads you to only admire the gown and wig without any academic effort, it is a waste of interest. Curiosity becomes a problem to mind of student when it becomes a pull and push to do and attempt evil. The picture of what you want to achieve is on the mind but you need caution to follow due process and order. Many students want success in examination at all cost, this led them to malpractice and they were caught – expulsion from school is the result.

Indiscretion

When curiosity is bad, student will develop **Indiscretion** in the mind. Curiosity is bad first, when it is indiscreet. Indiscretion (carelessness), a fault that is committed above all with the eyes, can be likened to stealing the goods of others. It is indiscreet to read the letters/SMS of other persons without permission, to look at somebody's paper during examination, etc. A mother instructs her son not to pry into her bag. It would also be indiscretion to listen to the phone conversations of others, or in our technical age, to open e-mails or enter the private computer files of others. If you are doing these acts, stop it today.

Scandals

Curiosity is bad, second, when it is scandalous. It is scandalous when one looks at what is indecent, be it in movies or in photographs, books, magazines, phones and so on. Looking at such things is morally sinful. All these will block your mind from thinking right.

Informal Attempt

Curiosity is bad, third, when it suggests attempting sex before marriage, wanting to romance opposite sex to calm the sex move. Cohabitation is out of curiosity to be a family person before the time. Love romances are also dangerous traps by which the Devil snatches uprightness and purity of customs from lives, especially girls. Your life is bigger than all these social vices. Any wrong attempt will strangle your dream to a sudden and unprepared full house wife, small dad, or jobless man with liabilities. Mind fills with sex will not succeed in inventions.

Reading of Anything

Curiosity is bad, fourth, when a purpose is not known in reading just any book or information on the net. Quest for information should be guided and controlled. Too much of knowledge makes a man goes extreme against his/her faith and values. Education is good but it does not produce wrong ideas. Education has produced ideas that gave us good roads, refineries, technology, modern farming, etc. Reading of anything will deform your ability of building career. Beware! Mind that swallows anything will vomit rubbish for his/her generation.

Latest Intoxication

Fashion trends will never cease. As much as we live, latest dresses and dressing will keep thrilling the eyes. Anyone who cannot control his/her curiosity to have all will end up being trapped, indebted, valueless, and wasteful. Love for latest phones is curiosity to steal, borrow, attempt unlawful acts, etc. Those who top career and fulfill dreams from the universities to polytechnics are not intoxicated and unsatisfied ones. They manage curiosity. From my research, the modest, calm, contented and godly students with learning mind always win the best student awards every year in our tertiary institutions. Do not be anxious to get all these things now. When you get the license to your career, all of them will come to you with ease. Give one for one.

Occultism

Wanting to know the mystery of this world makes some students travel far into the dark side of the world. In the Bible, Eve desired to know more and she accepted counsel of Satan. Truly, there is power in this world. Curiosity can prompt one to join witches, sorcerers, and fraternities in order to have influential words, power, and affluence and influence to show the world. All these start from the unguided mind. How many cult members actually get to the top of their career or invent a device? I was once in a tertiary institution where the cult big boss gave me open license to join them without being beaten as their rituals. Because I know where I am going, I refused the offer.[xli] When you get admission, people around you will share the good of such societal groups with you so that you can belong. As soon as you accept the offer, you have accepted to set your career ablaze mercilessly. Your dream career is bigger than short time influence, only within the school campus. You are destined to rule your world without weapons of war but with success and impact of your career. Think twice. Curiosity in the campus must not push you to such group. They are life-wasters.

Doing The Forbidden

In African culture, there are a lot of "don'ts" with consequences. I grew up to know some. I think they are African philosophical way of protecting lives from danger. But a curious person will attempt to see whether the consequence is real or not. Many had died because of that. If they escape the consequence, they move to do more and the sleeping dog of calamity is watching to strive at the tail time of life. This abomination is also forbidden by the Bible. Such forbidden acts are incest, tattoo, lesbianism, gay, street-fighting, cohabitation, act of disrespect, etc. In year 2000, a student fought his landlord publicly in my school. The act was dishonouring. Everyone could not stop the student because he thought he had physical strength. At the end, the old man showed him what is stronger than bone. He cast a spell on him and suddenly the student lost his consciousness and became imbecile. It was said that the student will continue to be an imbecile every date of that incident in every year, though he was healed. The fight actually led to riot that caused the school to be closed for a while. It is appropriate for a student to know his/her boundary. Don't attempt anything that can destroy your future and your career.

For Scientific Invention

However, curiosity can be managed positively. **For Scientific Invention** - When it is scientific, guided by prudence and Godly teaching with the aim of successfully interpreting the nature into things that will benefit human race e.g. discovery of medicine that cures diseases like Ebola,[xlii] HIV/AIDS; waste recycling; communication advancement; crime detector, etc. Invention requires curiosity. A good and praiseworthy curiosity was found in Andre Ampère who made great contributions to mathematics and chemistry; Alessandro Volta, inventor of the voltaic battery; Louis Pasteur, famous for his breakthroughs in microbiology, and other great minds in the world of invention. Every science student supposes to be curious of new discovery during JETS Club in the school.

Professional Duties

Some **Professional Duties** – A police officer or detective – will be curious to gather information that will resolve a matter. Such curiosity is timed and useful to save the innocent and punish the offender. A journalist will be curious on a story that will get the public informed. Auditor and accountant will be curious on "why an account is not balanced". Develop a good curiosity towards your career as from today. For curiosity can occupy all your time. Lastly, curiosity **to know God** makes us adherent to our faith. We grow to know God out of healthy curiosity.

Problem two – Laziness

A lazy mind is less than one person. Any student who is lazy cannot think for the nation, talk less of himself. The problem of physically sound but poorly-driven energetic person is laziness. Vision is good but accomplishment is the task. Great inventors never sleep much. They do much than what you price their invention. Some philosophers also wrote on laziness. A lazy student says, "It was such a lovely day I thought it was a pity to get up" (Somerset Maugham -1874 - 1965),[xliii] "Says little, thinks less, and does—nothing at all, faith" (George Farquhar -1678 - 1707),[xliv] "We grow old more through indolence, than through age" (Christina - 1626 - 1689).[xlv] Mind works as long as you engage it. A student who desires bright future will work harder both day and night. "I have a dream" is the song of many but "I have no input" is the enemy. A mind is a terrible thing to waste, so keep yours. Like most everything else in your body, your brain (mind) works all round the clock to save humanity. Do you know that a lazy man is a murderer? How? Many lives whose fortunes and safety are attached to his discovery die mercilessly. When you refuse to do one thing, you lose the opportunity of that moment.

God is perfect. He gives wisdom to anyone whose hands are strong to carry out His plans. Lazy man is a minus in the creation. Are you one of them? A lazy student depends on someone who uses his/her mind well. When I was in higher institution, I discovered some ladies used to flock with young men when the examinations come around the corner. Though they were beautiful, cute and always charming but they could not attempt any examination alone. Beautiful face has not invented anything. Only a beautiful mind does. Why do you accept mediocrity among other brilliant student in the school? I do always talk to myself that "I am not born to applaud others who make things happen but to be singled out among the crowd for excellence."[xlvi] Laziness whispers mediocrity within your mind that education is without stress. Mind of student attempts to step up grade above average. I challenge you to step up your grade in this term. If you do, then laziness is conquered.

Laziness cripples the mind. A lazy man buries his hand in the bowl, and will not so much as bring it to his mouth again.[xlvii] When the mind is weakened by indolence, the body will also respond to the effects. The eyes will be dull and dim to reading; hands will be short to carry out research; and the legs will be crippled to go to library, study room, classroom or tutorial centers for further studies. This is a problem you must conquer. How? Be determined to do what your mind prompts you to do. Do not delay your attempt. It may be too late. If your mind is willing, your body will gain strength to move on. Bible even says that, "The spirit indeed is willing, but the flesh is weak."[xlviii] The mind of student is highly endowed with invisible strength that can push on a weak body for long hour reading. You can read even when you are bodily weak. It is the matter of your strong mind. Laziness must not deny you your position at the top. Re-arrange your room, talk to yourself and position your mind for action. Each semester should have a new target that will strengthen your mind to work harder. First class is not an inheritance of some people. You can have it when your mind is ready for it. To conquer laziness, confess that you're lazy. This is sincere humility and true test for mind of student. Avoid delegating or depending on anyone what you can do. Prioritize your duties and do not procrastinate/postpone immediate task for other days, for it will become burdensome.

Problem three – Distraction

Mind has one major enemy. It is called distraction. When you run to where people say there is divine hand (malpractices miracle centers), you travail in pity and doubt because of distraction–which means distant attraction. A student with distractions will have noisy mind–noise of quick ambition, baseless vision, narrow thoughts, day dreams, complaints, argument, imaginations, bitterness, envy, hatred and disagreement. Distraction comes in disguise. In the school, students are exposed to things that can exchange their future for fun. This distraction can be in form of love making among the students, cultism, fashion madness, social media cravings, beauty competitions, extra curriculum activities, sporting activities, friendship, business opportunities, foods, music, lottery/gambling, reading romantic novels, partying, unguided travelling, addiction to seasonal movies, naughty political ambition, too much sleep, unguided group studies, uncontrolled religiosity, etc. Mind is too simple that it can be crowded and lost its focus. Watch out for irrelevant things that jam-packed your mind. Distraction will not allow you to think right. All the events will claim space in your mind. Master the tricks of distraction. They enter your mind through the body gates–eyes, mouth, ears, skin (touch), nose and heart (imagination).

Love making is emotional. It evolves the mind with the picture of the beloved either when you are conscious or subconscious. Love is for mature minds. It requires responsibility. If you are not ready for it, do not think about it. Bible says, "I charge you, O daughters of Jerusalem… of the field, do not stir up nor awaken love until it pleases."[xlix] Love comes with affairs. What is an affair? Affair means issue, matter and concern about totality of another person; not even self. Mind of lovers gives no space for other things. If you are still in secondary school, do not venture into love making. Even in tertiary institution, love dating has time. Some people that have target will first complete one before another. Wait till your mind has enough space to accommodate love.

Other distractions should be outlined and scrutinized on the basis of positive effects on your goal as students. Some distractions are not totally bad such as music, foods, extra-curricular activities, sporting activities, friendship, business opportunities, travelling, political ambition, sleep, group studies, religiosity and others. However, if it does not contribute to your dream, delete or delay till you are ready for it.

Problem four – Peer pressure

This generation is living in a postmodern world. The students of this age believe in themselves. They form clique to ruminate and share ideas, pains, experience and fun. Peer group starts from choice of friendship that you accept from your mind. Some will say, "My mind does not go with this fellow but this one". Peer group breeds peer pressure. Young adult encounter pressure. Pressure is a mechanism that grips the mind with force to take a step according to the dictate of others. Peer pressure can change a student mind if you allow it to grow. It is systematic. It starts on the day you accepted the friendship of a bad fellow; the day you craved after evil lifestyle; and the day you ignored your parent's advice. Though some parents cause the pressure in the mind of students. Every child wants self-respect, self-esteem and dignity of being human. Parents can correct their child indoor and must avoid public scolding.[1] If not, it will not correct the error but only harden the child. If a parent places curses, abuses and public insult on a child when he/she is with his/her peers, it will reduce morale and activeness of such child. The child will later do everything to avoid the parent's presence, deny parental link and want to stay out-door such as: extra days in the hostel/campus, seeking holiday elsewhere or bolt-up within the house. If you are a victim, do not sell you mind to friends. Seek reconciliation with your parents.

Peer pressure has made a brilliant student who used to lead the class to poor performance. Peer group is formed to share and counsel one another according to their level of knowledge which may not be totally correct. They bolt up against elderly advice. Though "Old school" counsel is old, but it is tested, trusted and proactive. You need an elderly person around you. A journey of fifty years with pitfalls can be shared within fifty minutes to save you from the same pitfalls. Mind of student who wants to learn will seek experiential counsel. Peer pressure can cause irreparable and irreversible damage. Let me share a story of a girl[li] who listened to wrong counsel from wrong peers. This young damsel was born into a Christian home where the parents supported their children's education, moral and physical life. This girl passed her entrance examination into secondary school. She lived in the hostel. As time went on, she started keeping secret away from her parents. She had love affairs with a boy which one of her friends introduced to her. She fell into sexual immorality as the friends taught her. She had to abort for the first time when the fear of early motherhood gripped her. Her parents called but she kept all secret. Until she had the fifth abortion that almost killed her, she never opened up. She had night mare, heavy minded, absent mindedness, and later failed her promotional exanimations. She later opened up when all hope was gone. The friends graduated from the school for tertiary institutions but she was asked to withdraw from the school. What a pathetic story! Run from friends that change clothes like chameleon without any source of income - they are aristos. Flocking around guys may earn you fame and popularity; that is the only fame you can ever have. You need to understand the distinctiveness of friendship before you get yourself involved. I had a story of some boys who left school to Lagos beach to compete on swimming.[lii] After the competition, one returned home while others drowned into the sea of no return – what a wasted destiny!

Problem five – Loss of interest

Mind and interest are friends. We learn because we have interest. Some students can watch seasonal movies for twenty-four (24) hours without missing a scene. It is the work of interest. We choose course base on interest. When interest on a thing is gone, no one can convince the fellow. Education cannot survive without the value of interest, for it keeps students in the class. Teacher impacts because the students show interest. Then, how does interest become problem in the mind of student? Interest starts from the mind and learning will take place. Interest sustains learning to get to discovery and invention level. Loss of interest must be managed. Students can lose interest in: a course, teacher, teaching style and learning environment.

If you hate a teacher, the interest level will drop and learning will not take place. Why do students hate teachers? First, when a teacher is impartial in his relationship among the student. Second, if he/she lacks proper lesson delivery. Third, the vulgar or foul language of the teacher to the student can make student to lose interest. Lastly, the presence of cane or the process of disciplining the students can create fear. I pulled out of Government class when I was in secondary school because I did not like the teacher.[liii] He used to throw any objects on students; he used to eat 'Kulikuli' in the class and he behaved wildly. Many of us left the class for another course because of our safety. Frankly speaking, if you lose interest because of these reasons, you are moving away from your goal. Today, I realized my mistake that I should have overlooked the error and understood his peculiarity. However, the teacher is not losing anything. Discipline is part of learning. Adaptation to teacher style of teaching is important. Good relationship with the teacher also enhances interest in the course.

To sustain interest, outline good reasons to be in that class. You must like the teacher as much as you can. Go extra mile into library to research more about the course/subject. Watch documentaries on the subjects and join group discussion class; it will help you remain alive in the class. Mind of student will strategize to keep interest alive no matter the inconvenience. Loss of interest on a subject can be as a result of self-error. When you flock together with wrong peers into a new class that you have no knowledge about, your interest in the subjects will drop. Other reasons are: Inability to interpret the connectivity of class with career; shallow knowledge about the subjects for your dream career; having secret agenda as students - social group, childhood friendship; flirting with opposite sex, etc.; if you manipulate yourself into a class through your parental influence, not your competence, the interest will surely fall; having hatred for some teachers in the new class; having wrong premonition about some subjects that they are difficult, all these will strangle interest in your mind. Have a pure mind towards your teacher, lecturer, course and the school. Do not study only what you have capacity for, study the difficult ones. Be real.

Every student can learn, just not on the same day or in the same way – George Evans

Problem six – Assimilating/understanding like others

Brain formation is by its capacity. God made us perfect with individual differences. Assimilation[liv] is an act of becoming part of something. It can be a learning process - the integration of new knowledge or information with what is already known. There is no dull student. We have lazy student, no doubt about that. What you learn is what you know. What you allow is what will stay. If you believe you can, then assimilation is possible. Our mind is wide and broad to accept as long as you believe you can. Immediate you cease to trust your capacity, assimilation drops. Some students are genius. They learn fast. If you do, do not look down on others. If you learn slowly, understand your uniqueness and write on your mind gradually without leaping like others. Those who invented what we use today were not born genius. They understood their peculiarity and developed approaches to learn best.

Mind of student learns at its pace. If you are a slow learner, be attentive in the class and visit library to read again what you learnt. Don't be shy to ask questions from the teacher during or after the class. It is a sign of the mind who wants to know better. Know your reading patterns and hours. Don't be 'copy and paste' student. Find out why a point is explained in that way. Be open to learn from anyone.

The noblest pleasure is the joy of understanding – Leonardo Da Vinci

Problem seven – Wrong decisions

Experience is the best teacher. Our mind programmes every actions, decisions and thought for years. Whenever a student makes wrong decision and it backfires, he/she will be skeptical to move on in that line. We live to make daily decision whether we like it or not. Nevertheless, we must make positive and guided decisions. Failure is blessing in disguise. Sam Adeyemi[lv] writes that dreams grow best in the fertilizer of failure. You can turn your failure into manure in which you plant the seed of new dream starting from your mind. He said and I quote,[lvi] "I have failed many times. I can write a good book on failure. In other words, I have tried many things that did not work, but I discovered that you can try ninety-nine ways that may not work for you, but one approach will eventually work out. The one that works will compensate for others that do not work". I strongly accept his worldview about failure. He who fails and refuses to try again is a failure. Because you fail a test, examination, interviews, assignment, group work or projects, does not hinder you from another trial. If you fail and you do not understand why you fail, then your decisions to do it again will be wrong.

Decision at a time like this needs courage. Many do not take courageous action because they do not want to die, but as the proverb says, "Cowards die many times before their death". If you die taking right decision, we shall remember you for life. Michael Catt in his book, *Courageous Living*,[lvii] says that there is a world of difference between standing at a grave and saying, "What a life" and standing at a grave saying, "What a waste." What will you be remembered for? How will you be remembered for? Face your Goliath as a prepared David with right stones. Do not surrender to fate. Avoid being a waste. You can do it again.

Problem eight – Financial interruption and embarrassment

Schooling without financial support wearies mind whenever the defaulters are exempted from school activities and examinations. I have seen the students in this situation. It is like a hole in the heart. They wish to have uninterrupted learning but they do not. At this time, mind will travel round the world for solution and whatever falls on the radar of the mind may be applied. Be careful to act fast. Be patient. Some students go into prostitution, aristos, arm robbery, pocket picking, kidnapping and online fraudulence. Few others may honourably embark on petty trade within and outside the school. All these are stressful for the mind of student who wants to learn. Learning with stress is like eating while running. Schooling with full support needs planning. I want you to sincerely answer these questions numbered below.[lviii]

1. Do you have supporting parents/guardians?
2. How supporting are they from cradle?
3. Do you support yourself sometimes?

4.   Do you have good relationship with your parents/guardians?
5.   Do they have a career of their choice for you?
6.   Do you have idea of bills to complete the training for the career?
7.   How buoyant are the parents/guardians?
8.   Have they promised to support you to any level of education at all cost?
9.   Are they pleased with your academic performance?
10. Are they pleased with your attitudinal character at home?
11. Do you choose career because your friend's parents/guardians are rich?
12. Do you have single parent or co-parent (both are divorcee)?
13. How cooperative are your parents/guardians to your education?
14. Do they have other viable means of raising money for your education?
15. Have you considered the stress of footing bill of such career before you chose it?
16. Do parents/guardians have savings for your education?
17. Are there any family members of parents/guardians that can assist?
18. Do you have any calculative and pragmatic plans of support for yourself?
19. Do you believe in God's help?
20. Do you know of any scholarship grants for career development in your country?
21. Have you considered learning a trade/entrepreneurship to support your career during training?
22. What can you do to earn more money without affecting your training?
23. What is your plan B when parental-support role fails?

If you have answers to these questions, your mind will be at rest 50% before you start your schooling. This problem is temporary. Adjust your bills. Do not be luxurious like other students. Cut your clothe according to your cloth/size. You can save your meager gifts to assist your parents. May God grant us uninterrupted schooling with rest of mind. Amen.

Problem nine – Religiosity

Religion begins from the heart (mind). Religion is the attempt of man to please God. Nevertheless, some students take over religion (excessively, sentimentally or affectedly) pious (disapproving) on their head. When you go to school to learn, you have opportunity to learn in the chapel/mosque and also in the classroom/lecture room. The extra commitment that makes you fanatic can affect your learning. Every religion has rules, time and pattern. You do not use the time of religion for studies and vice versa. The moment you are swapping lecture time for chapel programme, you are promoting hypocrisy. God is orderly in His approach. Church activities should move you closer to God and not to draw you away from your education. Wisdom is profitable. I had experienced of this matter when I was an executive in a campus fellowship. I managed the duo for excellence. But there was a sister in my class who attended the fellowship together with me. She was committed and faithful to fellowship programme but she was not doing well academically. We had final examination. I passed but she failed and had carry-overs.[lix] Religiosity must be managed as a student, so that your mind will not be weary to assimilate. Love God. Pray and attend programme, not every day, for it will backfire. Even when I was in seminary,[lx] we have chapel time. Library was closed while we worshipped. My advice: Live a balanced life that strengthens the mind with good conscience that will please God and lean better.

Problem ten – Inferiority/mediocrity

Inferiority[lxi] means lower in standard - lower or low in rank, standing or degree. It means–not as good: lower in quality or value; and mediocre - failing to meet a standard of quality, ability, or achievement. In Alfred Adler analysis of individual development, Adler stressed the sense of inferiority as the motivating force in human life. According to Adler, conscious or subconscious feelings of inferiority (to which he gave the name inferiority complex), combined with compensatory defense mechanisms, are the basic causes of psychopathological behavior.[lxii] It is an overdeveloped sense of being inferior to other people. In extreme cases, it can manifest itself in either withdrawn or aggressive social behavior. A student who looks down on himself will be inferior to any other person. God created dignity and regard for human life in our mind. Yet you must keep away from others because you think you are not at pal–relationship is unavoidable. Mind of the student does not tolerate inferiority. What others do, if you develop yourself, you can do better. Many students run from other colleagues because of clothing, eloquence, spoken of English language and having lowest scores in the class. All these points do not reduce your future worth, if you accept and develop yourself deliberately.

What you know - *knowledge*. What you can do - *ability*. What you prefer most - *choice*. All knowledge, ability and choice make you. Everyone has preference based on personal interest and value. Your uniqueness must not be traded away in career choice. You can admire others but do not lose yours. The point of uniqueness starts when everyone applauds you for an activity. Your uniqueness can win or lose. It is not a total failure, that's your uniqueness. Whenever you make progress in what you know best, do not laugh but smile. Whenever you fail despite your effort, do not cry but be frank. Sit down and research why the progress, so that you can monitor and master the pace. Your failure also needs investigation to know the weak point to be strengthened. What others do and fail, you can do it and be successful. Do not compare yourself to lose taste of your uniqueness.

Inferiority complex is loss of uniqueness – identity. Your mind says "You are nothing", "You cannot do it because you are fat", etc. When I was born, my parent rejoiced, for a unique child arrived. I grew in my own way. I talked as I wished; so you did. Let no one frustrate you against what you are and you can be. Your ability to manage your uniqueness is an indicator of success. Ask yourself these questions:[lxiii]

1. Do you prefer your gender?
2. Do you find fault in your physique?
3. Do you know how much you know?
4. Have you been honoured for your uniqueness among many others?
5. Do you compare yourself with others to appraise or condemn?
6. Can you list what you can do without anyone guiding you?
7. Are you happy to see yourself at the top of your career as you are today?

If you do, then you are unique specie of successful professional in the class of career. Mind of student sometimes feels not belong and therefore, it'll look for societal group to belong in order to raise his/her morale. I know you have what others do not have. What you think is nothing, is what someone is dying for. Sometimes you are unsatisfied with your life, while many people in this world are dreaming of living your life. It is like an analogue given by Doctor Ben Carson, Retired world renowned neurosurgeon that a child on a farm sees a plane fly overhead and dreams of flying. But, a pilot on the plane sees the farmhouse and dreams of returning home. That's life!! Enjoy yours. Wanting to belong is a cheat on your personality. I read a book that instilled courage and acceptance in my personality. It was written by co-authors and couple, Mike and Amarbel Ubi, *Why Singles Mingle*. Mike[lxiv] narrated his plight when he wanted to belong. He wrote, "I was in my teen, very naughty but my mother saw me as very good and obedient boy because I conducted myself very well whenever she is around. I had a friend who was probably years older than I, he was very wild, at the age of 15years, and he was already sleeping with prostitutes.

One day, he told me of a party. I got dressed up as if I was going to school but I had extra cloth in my bag; never got to school on that day, just to feel the heat of pleasure. For the first time in my life, on the way I was given a packet of cigarette and I knew I was going to smoke and probably sleep with a prostitute, deep down in my heart. I was not comfortable with situation but I could not back out on the journey. I knew the consequence it would amount to but God save me; though I was not a believer. What happened? As we moved along the road to the party, I was knocked down by a taxi, in fact the last word I heard was *'O ti ku'* meaning he is dead. I woke up in the hospital with my body covered with blood. After the incident, I vowed never to go anywhere with bad friends." When you feel below average, your mind may be polluted. God made you complete. Do you believe that? Yes, I do.

Problem eleven – Loss of determination

Great inventors never loosed grip of their dreams. They conscientiously determined to get it all. Determination is difficult to establish in the mind of student. But as soon as it finds a seat, only death can unseat it. Discouragement is the opposite of determination. People will discourage you. Friends will laugh at you as you read tirelessly in the library. Parents may not see your dream. Nevertheless, determined minds care less about external distractions. What is your dream? How do you conceive the dream? Your answers should give you a standing determination to realize the dream. This world is full of three set of people: those who watch things happening; those who appreciate/applaud things; and those who make things happen. I wish you be the latter. Be determined to change history and make a better history. Africa consumes and does not produce. System of education, state of tertiary institutions, inadequate infrastructure and lots more inadequacies must not stop your dream. Let's examine possible African discouraging syndrome.

Political and professional corrupt practices:

Since the birth of Nigeria, the tussle to lead the country fills the air and anyone wants to be part of the train and at the end acquire wealth and leave. Not only in politics, the professionals in companies and institutions also are guilty of corruption of any kinds. It is the normal system in Nigeria for dishonest people. All that should be used for development is spent on themselves and families. Anyone who comes up to sanitize the institution will be trapped unjustly. Nevertheless, you must purse your career to sustain positive change and honest practice. Be corruption-free.

Inadequate and old facilities for tertiary institutions:

Most universities and polytechnics have facilities that were installed from the premier point of the school. This challenge will surely affect career development for some students. The schools admit thousands of student to combat for the few and old facilities on ground. Nevertheless, you can still strive hard to be one of the best in the school despite the dilapidating of school structures. It is the matter of self-determination.

Incessant labour strikes:

The history of Nigerian schools does not complete without mentioning labour strike. This menace saps the students' energy to pursue career in Nigeria. It makes student to spend meaningless years in school than necessary. The labour Union fights for right. The government keeps promising, but the students keep suffering. Meanwhile many private universities have used the opportunity to gain ground and save the educational section from crumbling to dust. Nevertheless, you must keep your dream alive in this terrain, whether in public or private institutions.

Unstable educational policies:

Every time a new government emerges, new educational policies come up. It was 6.3.3.4 system before but now 1.6.3.3.4.[lxv] Every policy has gain and pain. It favours some people while others suffer. The old programmes of tertiary institution have not been reviewed to give room for modern development in career. Nevertheless, you need to read wide within and beyond curriculum. If policies change, you remain unchanged in your dream.

Blinking future:

The dream of anyone that pursues career is to practice one day. However, Nigerians with political power have hijacked the top with act of nepotism, bad policies and irregular structures. Many successful career men and women who have pledged loyalty to serve have fled the scene due to corrupt offer of inferior service for huge money. For example, a civil engineer knows what to do in constructing good road but the contract will be sideline and cut to penny and still expect good road. It is impossible. Nevertheless, you must stand your ground to sustain good service in your career.

No space for career youngsters on the top:

It is in Nigeria that old and potential retired workers refuse to leave the scene for young ones. After retirement, they still seek contract appointment. The career development needs upward flow from rear to the front. Nigeria has old and active professionals whose dreams are to outlive many generations. Nevertheless, you must strive hard to discover new things that will retire the old and allow the youngsters to appreciate intuition, discovery and invention in Africa. Do not lose your dream; be determined. You will get there.

Problem twelve – Wrong target

As I said earlier in chapter two, before you begin climbing up the ladder of success, make sure the ladder is leaning against the right building to avoid sudden fall. One of the very worst uses of time, I mean lifetime, is to do something very well that need not to be done at all. This is purely abuse of lifetime. Wrong target is also equal to waste of lifetime. Wrong target–wrong course, dream, and goal attract failure. Once you fail, it will melt your mind from doing another. Why did you choose what you chose? What do you want to achieve? Is it not for self-aggrandizement? Is the target visible and feasible? Possibility without sense is equal to impossibility. For every possibility has a layout plan to achievement. If the mind is set to roll out the script of your dream and you are equipped with wrong information, wrong friends, wrong aspiration and egocentric passion, such dream will fail. Wrong target must be avoided through proper planning, education and constant evaluation.

Problem thirteen – Modeling after wrong people

Modeling, mentoring and guidance must be managed. Our mind believes the counsel of anyone we choose to model, mentor or guide our lives. We see through their eyes. The mind of student learns from mentors. Praise George[lxvi] notes in his book, *Making It Work* that mentors are people who have done what you are trying to do. They have achieved what you are trying to achieve. Mentor or model can be from the past heroes, present inventors or close instructors in your school. However, caution must be in place to know the right counsel. Every student wants to learn new things with practicality from him who has done it. Not all models are model. Wrong mentor may instill wrong creed of individualism, immorality, atheistic power, and independent spirit in you. Some mentors, if you allow, may take away God from you and give you secularism. Beware!

Problem fourteen – Dreaming

Dreaming can be conscious and subconscious act. Every student dreams of tomorrow. The mind is the custodian of all dreams. If your dream is on white elephant, you may have dreamt impossibility. If you give yourself to dreaming without execution, you will be bored and believes that all dreams sleep in the mind of man. Day-dreaming is good and bad. It is psychological in nature. It may take away your rest, sleep and orderliness. I read a story of man who was day-dreaming of great tomorrow; I meant next day, when he would be awarded with medal by a white man. Ferdinand Oyono was the author, *The Old Man and The Medal.*[lxvii] The man was named Meka, he laid on bed waiting for sleep but the mind was heavily awake to see tomorrow. He began to imagine what the white man would do. He smiled alone. He thought about history of baboon. He smiled again and tried to form image of the white man he had never seen. "What martyrdom," he said out loud. "As soon as I have been given the medal I shall take off my shoes". It is a fun piece. When you day-dream too much, you will lose your mind to slight madness and your thought may not coordinate itself. Take your dream gradually with your pace. Success is metaphorical. You met some people on the way. You must follow the due steps to avoid stumbling to square one. Michael Faraday dreamt electricity but it did not work as he dreamt. He failed, tried and got it. Abraham Lincoln dreamt presidency but the dream encountered challenges yet he made it.[lxviii] If you give yourself to inadequate rest, your brain may retard in operation. Dream reality; not vague.

Problem fifteen – Health negligence

Sound mind is the result of sound health. Many students deliberately ignore the appeal of their body for good health at expense of reading and studying, to have all grades. Only the healthy brain can assimilate. Health involves good sleep, good reasoning, peaceful mind, strong bones, good blood pressure, etc. It all starts from your clean environments, personal hygiene and treatment of illness in time. Some students are dirtier than sewage centers. They do not sweep their living rooms, hotels, environments and rest rooms. A proverb says, "Cleanliness is next to godliness." And clean environment breaths good air. Campus, classroom, lecture room and rest rooms in the school should be hygienically cleaned to avoid germs, bacterial and virus that can break down immunity of students.

How often do you brush your teeth? It sounds funny. Do you bathe regularly? Bathing regulates your body temperature and instill calmness to the working brain. Do you eat balanced diet? Do you always go for junks? All junks and unhygienic foods may cause illness that will halt your studies and dreams. What do you use as make-up for your body? Some of them are cancerous (make-ups and skin-bleaching substances). I learnt a truth when a team of doctors and nurses came to my school on World Kidney Day[lxix] to educate the students and staff on the effects of what we use daily and how they can cause kidney diseases. The lecturer said that most creams with mercury cause damage to the skin.

Mercury is a dangerous and foreign chemical to the body and its presence is very harmful once it enters through the skin. Why? Skin regulates water pressure in the body and absorbs water into the body for kidney to sieve toxins from it. When the kidney overworks, it breaks down. I was opportune to watch television one day and I saw a young lady who just graduated from a university as Medical doctor, she was placed on dialysis to manage her kidney and water system in the body.[lxx] Her dream of future was gradually moving towards extinction because of the state of her health. Dream with health body. Only the healthy students' dreams come through.

Treatment of illness in time saves money, dream and life. Many students have lost their lives to negligence and impromptu treatment. Some even depend on self-medication. The more you delay your treatment, the more the danger of survival. Always visit the school clinic or family hospital to log complaint of your illness to a qualified doctor, not street chemist. Your future is costlier than the price of drugs you will pay in the hospital. As you grow, go for check up in the school sick bay, clinic or hospital, to know your Body Mass Index (BMI)–that is the relationship of your height with weigh to avoid obesity. Do exercise to avoid stress, overweight and boredom. Do not sit for long without stretching your muscles. Drink clean and adequate water for healing and smooth digestion. Avoid smoking, alcohol and hard drugs. Mind of real student cares for the body. Do you? Yes, I do.

Problem sixteen – Alcoholism and smoking
Alcoholism and smoking have power to influence your mind from right to wrong acts. Some student used to say or ask, "Is smoking a bad act?", "Does Bible mention smoking as evil?", "Is drinking of alcohol a sin?", "God created all things for our consumption", and "I drink but I do not drink too much". These are one and million statements and questions daily asked by students to justify the evil twin that affects human being. Some students always see these acts of drinking of alcohol and smoking as fun, pleasure, inspirer, confidence boaster, peace of mind sustainer

and significant addiction. Students are the victim of this menace. Let me talk about alcohol first.

Alcohol is made from the chemical called ethanol through fermentation process when bacteria react with sugar. The content is affected by how long it's left to ferment. If it is spirits, it goes through process of distillation to remove water and leave the stronger concentration for consumption as alcohol. Alcohol consumption can have numerous adverse effects on brain. It reduces communication between brain cells e.g. dementia – memory loss. Liver is vulnerable to damage by alcohol intake. It increases the risk of depression. It breaks home. It gives societal stigma. It becomes addiction. It mocks the drinkers.[lxxi] If affects ideal learning. Alcohol makes one poor. For the drunkard and the glutton will come to poverty.[lxxii] It rewards its victims with woes, sorrow, strife and wound without cause.[lxxiii] Alcohol makes a person to misbehave in the society – rape, disrespect, overconfidence, madness, etc.

Smoking is a popular activity for many people who continue to enjoy it even though they are well aware of the health risks. Bible does not mention smoking of cigarettes as a type of sin but it does attack it with scriptural application of truth. Smoking is evil against God. It is part of societal and civilized acts of sin. It affects body majorly because our body is the temple of God. Cigarette is made from tobacco which contains nicotine, a stimulant that affects both the mind and the body, and makes addictive. Nicotine is a powerful insecticide and a poisonous substance for the nervous system. There is enough (50mg) in four cigarettes to kill a man in just a few minutes if it were injected directly into the bloodstream. When nicotine reaches the brain in seconds, it stimulates the brain cells and then blocks the nervous impulse. This is where addiction to tobacco arises. Carbon monoxide (CO) that car produces when it fumes is 1.5%, but the smokers inhale smoke breathe in 3.2% of carbon monoxides directly from the source. Tobacco smoking has no less than 4000 irritating, suffocating, dissolving, inflammable, toxic, poisonous gases and substances in the smoke. As a cigarette is smoked, the amount of tar inhaled into the lungs increases. Tar is a mixture of substances that together form a sticky mass in the lungs. Carbon monoxide makes it harder for red blood cells to carry oxygen throughout the body.[lxxiv]

Smoking has numerous–dangerous–effect on man. Smoking kills quietly. It burns the lungs with carbon monoxide. It can lead to mental disorder. It affects the health status of a student living with risk of leukemia (blood cancer), coronary heart disease, risk of stroke, blood clots, and weakens blood vessel in the brain. Smoking changes structure of the skin, brown teeth, oral problems, mouth cancer, weak erection, early menopause, miscarriage, increases the risk of type 2 diabetes, kidney diseases and depresses appetite. It places tag on you in the public–school environment. Smoking can become addictive. If it is not stopped, it makes the students poorer (financially, mentally, spiritually and socially).[lxxv]

Smoking and alcoholism is sustained by addiction, i.e. the major problem that keeps students on as victims. Addiction is suggestive in nature; it tells you when to smoke and drink – an invisible colonial master. It becomes a routine act that you cannot stop. It presses the victim to do the acts at all cost. There will be no option for self-evaluation. Smoking and alcoholic drinking is difficult to detach from its victim. Addiction works with soul of a man (heart and brain). Devil strengthens its missions in man. Addiction is fueled with devil's cooked reasons to continue. Addiction has no shame. It does not respect any profession, e.g. Doctor smokes; he knows its effect yet he cannot stop it. Addiction has no budget. It consumes money against the health of its prey. It has no plan or purpose for living. Addiction enslaves its prey till the grave side. Addiction is not God's plan for man. God wants us to be free from this entanglement.

How can you be free from addition of alcoholism and smoking? Accept the life-changing grace of God through Jesus Christ. Believe in the healing power of God. Replace your addicted act with positive practice. Have positive reason for the stoppage. Avoid bad company – let your change be visible as you excuse old friends for Christ-minded ones. Daily read your Bible for guide and right decisions. Submit your worries to God. Pray all the time and whenever the urge for the sin comes, call on God, for He is right beside you to help. Tell others about your change of life and master your addiction. If you can do these, your mind will be free from stimulants that do not sustain confidence and morale for life. Addicted persons cannot become solution to the free ones. Free yourself first.

Problem seventeen – Excuse

"I was not the one who did it", "She was also their", "My mum was sick that is why I came late". All these excuses may be genuine but not tenable. Excuse is the human justification for wrong. When a student seeks to lessen the blame attaching to a fault or offence, he will hang on one excuse or the other. It is an explanation offered in the hope of being forgiven or understood. When do we give excuse? We use to present it when we fail; when we disappoint; or when we break law and order. Mind of student is not yet a perfect one, but it has room for procedural act of accepting blame for failure. When you fail, who should be blamed? Teacher, parents, government or yourself? Transfer of blame will not solve the problems. As student, be alive to see through and recognize your fault for improvement than shifting the fault to others. As a preacher says, "It is better you fail doing something than succeed doing nothing."[lxxvi] The statement was initially used in chapter two that "Whenever you make progress in what you know best, do not laugh but smile. Whenever you fail despite your effort, do not cry but be frank. Sit down and research why you progress so that you can monitor and master the pace. Your failure also needs investigation to know the weak point to strengthen".[lxxvii] It is the time to make up for your failure by digging deep the wrong actions that led to the failure i.e. – shallow reading, bad attendance, truancy, illness, etc.

Students give excuse for bad attitude like drinking of alcohol, prostitution, malpractice, cultism, etc. All these acts (indulgence) are not advisable for students who dream of better tomorrow. No matter the reasons, indulgence will surely harm your body, mind and dream. Humility is the only antidote for excuse. If your excuse grants you escape today, you will not prefer the pending consequences for tomorrow. Accept your wrong for right actions today.

Problem eighteen – Procrastination

Procrastination is the thief of time and opportunity. It involves delay strategy. Students have suffered diverse loss due to procrastination. We sometimes procrastinate reading, doing of assignment, going for research, attending lecture and the like. A student with mind to learn will endure the stress of one thing at a time. What must be done must not wait till another day. The strength and enthusiasm of today is never equal to another. Do you delay things that would bring you closer to your dream? I know you do. But why? You start a thing with purpose of completing it, suddenly other thing pops up and you drop the initial, you have cheated yourself that day. Some students read, take a break, read another novel, watch another TV show, etc. because they lack value for priority. Procrastination[lxxviii] excels in the mind of student who has fear of outcome. Whenever you get involved in complex task, procrastination will surely surface. Do your work gradually. Lack of motivation and focus permits the negligence. When there is fatigue, you will not be able to complete your work. Find time to relax and do your work completely.

Problem nineteen – Reading sickness

Malaria, typhoid, headache or stomachaches have drugs. They can be diagnosed by the precedent guidelines in medicine but reading sickness is difficult to diagnose and it's peculiar to students. Studentship is attained because of books we read. I wonder why library is always scanty in patronage. Students go to classroom to listen to teachers, lecturers and instructors but they do not develop habit of personal reading. What you read is what your mind shall conceive. That is why the caliber of graduate in our schools cannot defend their disciplines. The skills of oration and eloquence are fading away because students read to pass examination alone. Reading goes beyond the examination room.

You cannot open a book without learning something – Confucius

Readers are leaders and not all leaders are reader. You may not sit on the throne to lead but your contribution as a reader can guide the kings. When you read you take ideas from people to complement yours. A healthy student supposes to read at least four (4) hours per day. He/she will revise, review, do assignment and discover new thoughts. Reading at the time when the tests or examinations come closer is an aberration to studentship. Overloading of brain at the point of examination does not do any good to the student but evil such as abuse of brain, indigestion of thought (there will be breakdown in assimilation), volatility of points, ill-heath and migraine. Reading is the cheapest means to feed the mind with relevant tools for dream actualization. Visit the library for relevant and educational books. You can also visit online for current books. These are kind of books you need to read to feed your mind with knowledge:

Old books:
From the shelves of your parents or the old apartment/store/library of your neighbour/relatives/friends, there they keep logs of old books which can still inspire your thought. Some old books remain the primary source for the new books, i.e. most new books have their ideas from the foundation laid. You can still read them to know the pitfalls of that generation and the success story of her champions; for principles do not change, but the applications differ. You can also get these books on the street shops, old bookstores and online stores.

Free books:
This offer comes seldom. Some organizations are committed to free books through internet or via post. It may be in form of correspondence, magazine, or e-books. The danger of free offer is that the appetite to read such books is slim because it does not cost you anything; however, endeavour to overcome that.

Library books:
The organized stores with shelves of books for the purpose of reading when they are needed. It is not for decoration. Library can be in the church, national resource center, private resource centers, personal shelves and school library. Visit any of these centers to borrow or read books often than before.

Borrowed books:
These books are not your own. It means they are borrowed for a number of days from friends, school library, national or private library. Such books should be borrowed when needed, not for fun or decoration. It is good to read and glean down points so that the book is returned after it has completely served its purpose.

Online books:
There are a lot of books online; both old and new which you may not get within your city or country except by courier from another country. These books are stored electronically for download. It may be for free, by subscription, or limited preview. You can get them from:

- www.google.books.com
- www.amazon.com
- www.ebay.com
- www.lulu.com
- www.createspace.com
- www.kobo.com etc.

These books can be received through courier service or in pdf format on your computer. Books can also be in form of article split into pages on blog pages which has feedback mechanism from the reader to the authors and publishers of the webpage.

E-Books:
These books can be online, on kindle, smart phone, PC, etc. in format of pdf, ePub, and doc. You can download free books from these websites on any issues.

- www.educatorstechnology.com
- www.edsitement.neh.gov

- www.eyewitnesstohistory.com
- www.edmodo.com
- www.dosomething.org
- www.abcteach.com
- www.ala.org
- www.artsedge.kennedy-center.org/educators.aspx
- www.bartleby.com/usage
- www.readprint.com
- www.manybooks.net/about
- www.rarebookroom.org
- www.creativecommons.org
- www.freetextbooksonline.com
- www.textbookrevolution.com
- www.nou.edu.ng
- www.en.wikibooks.org/wiki/Main-page
- www.openculture.com/free_textbooks
- www.studentpirgs.org/open-textbooks/catalog
- www.en.classroom-aid.com/educational-esources/open
- www.etc.usf.edu/lit2go
- www.librivox.org
- www.gutenberg.org
- www.bookshouldbefree.com
- www.librarianchick.com
- www.learnoutloud.com
- www.en.childrenslibrary.org
- www.oxford.co.uk
- www.storyplace.org/storyplace.asp
- www.plcmc.lib.nc.us
- www.storytimeforme.com
- www.digilibraries.com
- www.archive.org
- www.openlibrary.org
- www.planetebook.com/free-ebooks.asp
- www.freereading.net
- www.teachinglibrary.co.uk
- www.k12opened.com/ebooks

- www.creativecommons.org/licenses/by/3.0/
- www.teacher.scholastic.com/commclub
- www.ams.org/bookstore
- www.feedbooks.com/publicdomain
- www.bookshare.org
- www.digitalindex.org
- www.classicreader.com
- www.e-booksdirectory.com
- www.sciyo.com
- www.4ebooks.org
- www.free-ebooks.net
- www.getfreeebooks.com
- www.freecomputerbooks.com
- www.freetechbooks.com
- www.scribd.com
- www.globusz.com
- www.knowfree.net
- www.onlinefreeebooks.net
- www.bookyards.com
- www.asksam.com/ebooks/
- www.baen.com/library
- www.ebooklobby.com
- www.freebook-s.com
- www.ebook-cafe.com

Bookshop:

Commercial shops for book selling. It is good and appropriate for an educated person to visit a bookshop at least once in a month to know which book is newly published in his/her field. Buy a book per month to equip yourself mentally and academically. Mind of student will always yearn for development as he reads. Your mind is the only healing and drugs against reading sickness. Be determined to read today.

Problem twenty – Truancy/absenteeism

It is an act of rebelling against authority figures by being absent from school. Truancy begins from the mind. When a teacher beats a student, such child may decide to forego the classroom for the teacher. I had this experience in my secondary school when a few students decided to abscond the formal classroom for an empty classroom as their common base to discuss movies, gamble, drink hard drinks and sleep. At the end, they repeated the class and a few others left the school because of the shame.[lxxix]

Problem twenty one – Home tussle

Every student emanates from home where father and mother exist. There are some exemptions such as: co-parenting (divorce home), single parenting, grand parenting and cohabitations. These kinds of homes have great influence on the mind of student in the school. I have seen student who was absent-minded in the class because of home tussle. The problem is not from the student but the parents who refuse to cooperate on the care of their children. Also, polygamous home writes strife and hatred in the mind of students where the mothers and the step mothers combat and abuse one another every morning. The level of concentration will surely diminish as long as the home is not friendly.

Some homes breed partiality, favouritism, war, hatred, poverty, enmity and lawlessness. They have counter effect on students' learning. I read a book by Joyce Meyer titled, *Conflict Free Living.*[lxxx] It was a life story in relation to her immediate family. She narrated, "I grew up in a violent and angry home, and my entire childhood was filled with fear, embarrassment, and shame. My father sexually, physically, verbally and emotionally abused me from the time I was three until I left home at eighteen. He never physically forced me to submit, but he did force me to pretend I liked what he was doing. He used anger and intimidation to control other family members and me. When I turned eighteen, I moved out of my parents' home while my father was away at work one day. Shortly after that, I married the first man who showed no interest in me. My first husband was a manipulator, a thief, and a fraud man who was usually unemployed. He once abandoned me with nothing but a dime and a carton of soda bottles". This is an example of home tussle that many students are experiencing on daily basis.

Another story from 'Bimbo Odukoya in *How to Handle Rejection*,[lxxxi] on a lady called Kate. She was still in her mother's womb when her father denied responsibility for her. Therefore the paternity was under question even as the unborn child. The father accused the mother of sleeping with someone else because it had been proven that he could not sire children. He remained adamant to the fact. After many years, people used to tell Kate that she resembled her father too much. The father showed her rejection and hatred. She had poor self-image and felt hopeless. I want to add that such lady will not be able to learn, assimilate or study in the school as long as she remembers her home.

If you belong to this kind of home, pray to God for your peace. Do not harbor hatred in your promising mind that has dream of great tomorrow. Forgive the wrongs of your parents and determine to build a godly home when you grow up for marriage. In your classroom, do not think about your family woes. Concentrate on your passion to discover new policy, invention, solution, laws and ideas that Africa is waiting for.

Education is the better safeguard of liberty than a standing army –
Edward Everett

Problem twenty two – Misuse of freedom

Teenagers and young adults want freedom. They crave for liberty of thought and expression. Yet there is due process for it. My greatest amazement of the students is the crave for independence at all cost. A child of ten years old is negotiating for privacy. I wish to share Mike and Amarbel Ubi's story again,[lxxxii] especially the incident that made Amarbel learnt a serious lesson of her life. She wrote, "I was very young and tender, I wanted to express myself like others but I lived with my mother. I was opportune to stay with my aunty in the city where I was enrolled back in school that's where I met Juli. As a teenager, I envied Juli, my friend because she had everything that I did not have. There was a day she wanted me to accompany her to a friend's place, I told my aunty that there was a get-together in the school after the closing hour; that I would be a little bit late from school. I accompanied her as agreed; not knowing it was her boyfriend's place. We met some other boys thee at our arrival, but later excused themselves and left the room, leaving behind my friend, her boyfriend, me and one of the boys who was supposed to be my toaster for the evening. It was a real setup. Before I knew it, the boy was already cuddling Juli on the bed while the other boy wanted to romance me while I was sitting on the chair. When I resisted him, he stood up and put off the light. I was terrified because of my aunty and mother's voice that echoed in my ears. I fought, jumped and escaped out of the room."

Education is the key to unlock golden door of freedom – George Washington Carver

Freedom is good but management of freedom is costly. As a student, enjoy and endure the rule and guide of your parent; it is for some times. Peer group always agitate for liberty to wear anything (nude), go anywhere (party), do anything (immoral), and express their opinion. Seeking for freedom blocks your sense of reasoning. Many secondary school students struggle to graduate and proceed to tertiary institution in order to express their right of liberty. It is true that you will need to think for yourself, yet you must remember your link with your family principle and values. Freedom always contends with external values. Why? Freedom likes to breed on its own. Let your religious belief and values that are needed for life be deeply engraved in your mind before you leave home for tertiary institution. Some parents will tell their child "Remember the son/daughter of whom you are".[lxxxiii] This statement has values, beliefs, principles and contentment embedded inside. Freedom can be guided if you intentionally allow yourself to be guided. You need to involve yourself in home duties such as cooking, cloth washing, environmental cleaning, car washing, room cleaning, bed laying, grass cutting, plate washing, etc. Do not ignore duties because you are boy or girl. All these will be useful in your tertiary education life and beyond. When freedom comes fully, you will be responsible children the parents can vouch and boast for without any regret. Do not allow freedom of expression makes your mid unruly to lecturers and teachers, and unguided towards your studies.

The only person who is educated is the one who has learned how to learn and change – Cart Rogers

Problem twenty three – Too know syndrome

Have you ever been absolutely sure that you were correct about something? Maybe your mind appeared to have all facts to prove you right–but you ended up being wrong. What did you do? Did you admit your error, or did you keep pushing and trying to find a way to defend your position? Joyce Meyer gave us a story of this syndrome "Too know". One evening she had a drive with her husband on visitation to a member's house. Along the way, the husband, Dave confessed that he did not remember the street and the house, but Joyce claimed she knew the house very well. Dave said, "I don't think that is the right way to go". Joyce persistently agreed she knew the way until they drove to where she said and found that it was a wrong address. She said, "I was wrong as wrong would be." [lxxxiv]

He who would learn to fly one day must first learn to stand and walk and run and climb and dance; one cannot fly in the flying – Friedrich Mietzsche

A student with this syndrome will lose confidence in himself after some years. It is better to learn patiently. 'Too know' student rarely sees others as equal. He believes in his competence. Even the teachers cannot correct such person. Over-confidence shall surely bring shame on that person. Mind of student should be humble to learn from others. Even when you know the answer, wait to hear from others first. 'Too know' student will not bother to read instructions before writing examinations. Be peaceful in your mind. Bend low to hear, learn and do according to instruction, not as you think it should be. Any embarrassment you receive after your mistake may discourage your mind to know more. Be warned!

Student's mind has many other problems but only few that were discussed in this chapter, should be able to guide your mind whenever such problems emerge. However, the mind that survives associated problems will surely solve societal problems. Read on.

CHAPTER FOUR
POWER OF STUDENT'S MIND

An idea that is developed and put into action is more important than an idea that exists only as an idea — Edward de Bono

A man may die, nations may rise and fall, but an idea lives on — John F. Kennedy

Power belongs to God and He gave the needed power to man when He breathed into Adam that day. Since the fall of man, power became issue of struggle among men. Yet the real power still resides in man who diligently understands the principle. Power of student's mind are not based on external influences–governmental authority—but influence that originates from creative ideas that can solve man's problem and make life better day by day. This power is in form of little but big idea to turn blackness to light, boredom to life, pain to comfort, etc. A great motivational speaker, Myles Munroe, in his book *God's big Idea*,[lxxxv] notes that the world is ruled by dead men. This statement may surprise you, but after a little thought, you would likely agree when you consider that all of the ideologies, rules, laws, theories and principles that serve the governments, medicine, technology, sociology, psychology, etc., are all born of ideas cultivated, incubated, and developed by men who, though long laid to rest, still live on in the practice of these ideas in modern societies. Theory of evolution by Charles Darwin (1859); theory of psychoanalysis by Sigmund Freud (1856-1939); federalism was first used by United State of America (1789); law of effect by Edward Thorndike (1874-1949); theory of gravitation by Isaac Newton (1687), etc. were formulated by dead ones who had served humanity. Does it mean you also cannot formulate a new theory for this age?

The whole purpose of education is to turn mirrors into windows — Sydney Jr. Harris

It is a pity that what our generation produces on daily basis is unscrupulous to human existence. We think extortion of resources, trading for warfare, corruption, terrorism and annihilation of innocent human life, slave trade, oppression, etc. I know one thing that God's good idea in man's mind will surely prevail one day. In your mind right now, are you stirred to discover solution to our world or continue to endure the servitude of wicked few who only lead to fill their belly and ruin the poor? Munroe[lxxxvi] still writes further that death can never kill an idea. Ideas are powerful than death. Ideas outlive men and can never be destroyed. The power of your mind cannot be destroyed as long as you discover it. The battle for this Earth is the battle of mind of thinkers that have ideas. The great heroes that used their mind to coin theories, laws, formula, government ideologies, etc. were born by ordinary parents like yours. They went to school as you do. They were ordinary with flesh and bones but extraordinary in their thinking for solution. They learnt under a teacher with a submissive mind to glean basic and foundation of knowledge. I believe in you too that you were born to excel, greater than these ones. Maybe if you read through the discoveries of these dead ones, you will be encouraged and stirred up for excellence. The record of inventors and invention with dates are detailed below.[lxxxvii]

I have leant that people will forget what you said. People will forget what you did, but people will never forget how you make them feel — Maya Angelou

350? BC - Aristotle Classifies Plants and Animals - Greek philosopher Aristotle establishes a taxonomy that recognizes two kingdoms of living forms, Plantae and Animalia. The concept of the two kingdoms remains intact for centuries.

330 BC - Aristotle Organizes Knowledge - Science as an organized system of thought begins as Greek philosopher Aristotle explains the physical world in a methodical way, proposing that the world is made of four elements (earth, air, fire, water), with four qualities (cold, hot, dry, wet), and four causes (material, efficient, formal, final).

300? BC - Herophilus Revolutionizes Anatomy - Greek physician Herophilus is the first to base anatomical conclusions on dissection of the human body. He recognizes the brain as the center of the nervous system, distinguishes motor from sensory nerves, and is the first to recognize that arteries contain blood, not air.

260 BC - Arabic Numerals Introduced - Hindus in India develop the Arabic system of number notation around 260 BC. This system introduces the concept of positional notation. It is probably introduced into the Arab world about the 7th or 8th century ad.

250? BC - Greek Inventor Ctesibius - Greek scientist and engineer Ctesibius, who resides in Alexandria, Egypt, constructs a catapult that propels missiles with forced air and devises the first musical organ. His other notable contribution to science is in improving the clepsydra, or water clock. He makes the water clock highly accurate by employing a floating rack that turns a toothed wheel.

240? BC - Eratosthenes Measures the Earth's Circumference - Greek scientist and philosopher Eratosthenes measures the earth's circumference using the position of the noon sun at summer solstice and the difference in latitude between two towns. His calculation is only about 15 percent too large.

240? BC - Archimedes Calculates Pi - Greek mathematician Archimedes first calculates the value of pi. Though the Greeks are not familiar with the decimal system, Archimedes' calculation is accurate to two decimal places.

215? BC - Archimedes Discovers Law of Hydrostatics - Greek mathematician Archimedes discovers the law of hydrostatics, which states that a body immersed in a liquid feels an upward force equal to the weight of the liquid displaced. This law is also called Archimedes' principle.

150? BC - Romans Develop Concrete - One of the most significant innovations in architecture occurs when the Romans discover a way of mixing pozzolana, a natural silicate, with pieces of brick and rock. The resulting concrete is lighter than stone and revolutionizes construction engineering.

105 - Paper Made in China - According to tradition, Ts'ai Lun, a eunuch attached to the court of the Chinese emperor Ho Ti, makes the first paper. He probably uses mulberry bark, making the paper on a mold of bamboo strips.

210? - Chinese Invent Wheelbarrow - People in China invent the wheelbarrow. It is used to haul dirt, rocks, and food supplies. Easy to push, it can be handled by one person.

250? - 900? - Maya Develop Highly Accurate Calendar - Maya priests of Mesoamerica create and maintain a sophisticated pair of interlocking calendars to help them plan ceremonies. One of the calendars is a 260-day religious almanac for determining lucky and unlucky days. The other is a standard 365-day calendar based on the movements of the sun. The calendars work in concert like geared wheels, with standard days periodically lining up with the days on the religious almanac.

386? - 419? - Jerome Translates the Bible into Latin - Christian scholar Jerome becomes governor of a monastery in Bethlehem, where he translates the Bible into Latin from Greek and Hebrew. This authoritative translation, the so-called Vulgate Bible, becomes the most common edition used in Europe during the Middle Ages.

1040? - Chinese Experiment with Gunpowder - Chinese writer Tseng Kung-liang publishes the first-known gunpowder formulas for use in three weapons: a bomb hurled by a kind of catapult, a bomb with hooks, and a poison-smoke ball.

1519 - Ferdinand Magellan Sails Around the World - Portuguese explorer Ferdinand Magellan is the first to cross the Atlantic and the Pacific Oceans in a single journey. He dies in a battle, but one of his ships completes the global circumnavigation, returning to Seville on September 6, 1522.

1543 - Andreas Vesalius Founds Modern Anatomy - Belgian anatomist and physician Andreas Vesalius publishes De Humani Corporis Fabrica and establishes the foundations of modern anatomy. His dissections of the human body and descriptions of his findings help correct misconceptions in existence since ancient times.

1597 - Plastic Surgery Textbook - Italian surgeon Gaspare Tagliacozzi, who pioneers modern plastic surgery, publishes the first textbook on the subject. Plastic surgery is one of the oldest forms of surgery practiced, but is improved considerably in the 16th century.

1608 - The First Telescope - Dutch lens-maker Hans Lipperhey discovers that a distant object appears to be much closer when viewed through a concave and convex lens held in front of each other, and invents the first telescope.

1609? - Galileo is First to Use Telescopes in Astronomy - Using a homemade telescope, Italian scientist Galileo discovers the four moons orbiting Jupiter, the rings of Saturn, and the phases of Venus. Galileo is the first person to use a telescope for the scientific observations of astronomical objects.

1611 - King James Version of Bible is Published - James I of England commissions a revision of the English Bible, a 14th-century translation by John Wycliffe. The King James Version, as it is called, is completed in 1611.

1618 – 1621 - Kepler Explains the Orbits of Planets - German astronomer Johannes Kepler publishes Epitome of Copernican Astronomy over a three-year period. The book consolidated many of his discoveries, including his three laws of planetary motion.

According to Kepler's laws, the planets revolve around the Sun in elliptical orbits at varying speeds. This work influences astronomers for many years to come.

1684 - Invention of Calculus - German mathematician Gottfried Wilhelm Leibniz publishes an account of his discovery of calculus. The English physicist and mathematician Sir Isaac Newton developed calculus independently in 1666 but does not publish a description of his method until 1687.

1687 - Isaac Newton Discovers the Law of Gravity - English scientist and mathematician Sir Isaac Newton derives the law of universal gravitation. This discovery, considered one of the greatest intellectual achievements of modern science, explains how an unseen force known as gravity affects all bodies in space and on earth. Newton publishes his findings in *Philosophiae Naturalis Principia Mathematica* in 1687.

1698 - Thomas Savery Invents the Steam Engine - English engineer Thomas Savery builds the 'Miner's Friend,' the first practical steam engine, which serves as a water pump. It uses two copper vessels alternately filled with steam from a boiler.

1796 - Smallpox Vaccine - British physician Edward Jenner develops a vaccine against smallpox, a major cause of death in the 18th century. His work lays the foundation for the science of immunology.

1804? - First Practical Locomotive - British inventor and engineer Richard Trevithick constructs the first practical steam locomotive in 1804. Within fifty years the railroad becomes the dominant means for moving people and freight.

1837 - First Telegraphs - American inventor Samuel F. B. Morse and British physicist Sir Charles Wheatstone (the latter in collaboration with British engineer William F. Cooke) independently invent the first electric telegraphs.

1842 - German physician and physicist Julius Robert von Mayer formulates the law of conservation of energy, later known as the first law of thermodynamics. German scientist Hermann von Helmholtz and British physicist James Prescott Joule also are credited with discovering this principle.

1839 - Cell Theory Proposed - German botanist Matthias Schleiden and German zoologist Theodor Schwann, working together, recognize the fundamental similarities between plant and animal cells and propose that all living things are made up of cells.

1858 - Darwin's Theory of Evolution - English naturalist Charles Darwin announces his theory of evolution through natural selection at the same time that English naturalist Alfred Russel Wallace independently devises a similar theory. Darwin's complete theory is published in On the Origin of Species in 1859.

1865? - Basic Principles of Genetics - Using varieties of garden peas, Austrian botanist Gregor Mendel works out the basic principles of genetics. His theory of dominant and recessive genes is published in an obscure journal.

March 10, 1876 - First Telephone - Using a transmitter and receiver he had constructed (and for which he had received a patent three days previously), Scottish-American inventor Alexander Graham Bell delivers the first telephone message to his assistant, Thomas A. Watson.

1877 - Internal Combustion Engine - German inventor Nikolaus A. Otto patents the Otto cycle engine. It is the first effective four-stroke internal combustion engine, the type that will eventually be used in automobiles.

1873 - Electromagnetic Theory of Light - British mathematician and physicist James Maxwell publishes his electromagnetic theory of light and suggests that a whole family of electromagnetic radiation must exist, of which visible light is only one part.

November 05, 1895 - X Rays Discovered - German physicist Wilhelm C. Roentgen discovers a form of electromagnetic radiation he calls X rays. With these emissions, which have shorter wavelengths than light, he produces an image of the bones of his fingers.

December 17, 1903 - First Airplane - At Kitty Hawk, North Carolina, American aviator Orville Wright makes the first successful flight of a piloted, heavier-than-air flying machine. Built by Wright and his brother, Wilbur, the craft flies a distance of about 37 m (120 ft).

1919 - First Artificial Nuclear Reaction - British physicist Ernest Rutherford bombards nitrogen gas with alpha particles and obtains atoms of an oxygen isotope and protons. This transmutation of nitrogen into oxygen is the first artificially induced nuclear reaction.

1926 - Theory of Wave Mechanics - Austrian physicist Erwin Schrödinger presents his theory of wave mechanics, which expresses Louis de Broglie's 1923 wave concept mathematically. He is awarded the 1933 Nobel Prize in physics for this work.

1930? - First Jet Engine -British aviator and aeronautical engineer Sir Frank Whittle files his first patent for a turbojet engine. It is more than a decade before the first flight powered by the engine takes place, however. The engine is tested in a British experimental fighter plane during World War II.

1944 - DNA as Basis of Heredity - Canadian-born American bacteriologist Oswald T. Avery publishes a paper outlining research showing that the agent responsible for transferring genetic information is not a protein, as biochemists had believed, but the nucleic acid DNA.

1948 - Transistor Invented - American physicists Walter H. Brattain, John Bardeen, and William B. Shockley develop the transistor, a solid-state electronic device consisting of a tiny piece of semiconducting material. The transistor replaces the vacuum tube in computers and calculators, and the three scientists share the 1956 Nobel Prize in physics for their work.

1957 - Fortran Developed - A team headed by American mathematician John Backus develops Fortran, the first high-level computer language. It allows people to write programs in mathematical terms rather than in machine language.

April 12, 1961 - First Human in Space - Soviet cosmonaut Yuri Gagarin becomes the first human to travel in space. Launched aboard Vostok 1, he orbits Earth once, spending an hour and 48 minutes aloft.

December 03, 1967 - First Heart Transplant - A team headed by South African surgeon Christian Barnard transplants the heart of a 25-year-old woman into a 55-year-old man, who dies of a lung infection after 18 days.

July 20, 1969 - First Moon Landing - U.S. astronauts Neil Armstrong and Edwin "Buzz" Aldrin, Apollo 11 crew members, become the first people to walk on the Moon.

1971 - First Microprocessor - In 1969, American engineer Marcian Edward (Ted) Hoff proposes the idea of putting all of the logic circuitry of a calculator's central processing unit on a single chip. This first microprocessor, which Intel produces in 1971 and names the Intel 4004, leads to many of the major computer developments of the following decades.

1975? - First Personal Computer - The first personal computer, the Altair 8800, is introduced. Developed by American electronics engineer Edward Roberts, it has 256 bytes of memory and is an instant success.

1982 - Prions Discovered - American neurologist Stanley P. Prusiner discovers proteins called prions, which are linked to brain disorders in mammals. This discovery contradicts long-held assumptions that only agents with DNA or RNA, such as viruses and bacteria, can replicate in the body and cause disease.

1983 - AIDS Virus Identified - Scientists led by French cancer specialist Luc Montagnier isolate a previously unknown retrovirus from the lymph node of a man at risk for what becomes known as the acquired immune deficiency syndrome (AIDS). It is recognized as the cause of AIDS.

Genius is an African who dreams up snow — Uladimir Nabokov

These great minds, their works are still useful for our generation. We build on the foundation. What will you discover or build on that will write your name on the rock of history? The power of the mind of student resides in the brain. I discussed slightly on brain in chapter one. Now there is need to know why great heroes of inventions excelled. Did they have different brain from yours? Or did they do something else that you have never done or known? Let's study together.

Brain of the Genius That Invents New Things

Students are created by God with diverse and perfect abilities: intelligence and creativity. These are generally regarded as highly valuable assets of human mind. Some called it Intelligence Quotient (IQ), while others called it being genius. What is intelligence? Intelligence[lxxxviii] is problem solving ability. It has ability to process issues in the mind. When you hear about someone in your class or neighbourhood who has problems, how do you feel? Does your reasoning start working immediately to proffer solution? Or the mind in you keeps quiet unbothered? Solving problem is a peculiar attribute of genius. They lose their peace when they see problem unsolved. In 2014 when Ebola disease struck Nigeria and other West Africa countries, how did you feel? Did you process abstract solution within? The potential geniuses will start to read, study, pass exam and seek admission for course that will solve the problem in the nearest future. In the classroom, how do you reason along with your teacher? Genius sees problem ahead and processes solution in form of questions. Nobody is a dull student. It is your decision. If you engage yourself, you will produce result.

Genius is talent set on fire by courage — Henry Van Dyke

Albert Einstein was a genius. So were Leonardo DaVinci, Bobby Fischer, Nikola Tesla, Marie Curie, Ludwig van Beethoven, and

Madame Da Stael. Why are these individuals considered geniuses? What measures are we putting together to determine this? Certainly, these individuals had contributed to our society, whether scientifically, or culturally. But what makes a genius? Are the brains drastically different from non-geniuses or normal people? There are four differences discovered. They are: connections; the thalamus; gray matter; and the approach.[lxxxix]

Connections[xc] have to do with relative equal spilt between the long and short connection of the cerebral cortex within the brain. It speaks volume of interest level of the mind over a thing or many things. Short connection is correlated with aptitude pertaining to something that interests us, while long connection pertains to our capacity for things outside of these interests. The connections in genius split between long and short connections leans heavily towards one another. For example, Beethoven (a musician) probably had a great deal of short connection, pertaining to musical ability alone. Someone like Blaise Pascal most likely had a larger amount of long connections in his cortex since he was highly accomplished in everything from mathematics to prose to theological philosophy. Anyone with short connection has interest in one thing. They develop deep passion on just one thing. Are you also enthusiastic about one thing? Take time to research, develop and discover more as a student. The long connection builds student with multiple talents. They can do many things. Their composition makes them all-round useful persons. If you are one, be calm and creative.

The thalamus, the brain filter, is essentially determined what gets through the brain. This receptor is like a bottleneck that filters what goes into the brain.[xci] It allows valuable information to proceed for processing. In normal brain, the bottleneck is narrow, most likely, not going to reach conscious thought. In genius brain, the receptor tends to be wider, letting more thought come though. Do you read to reason over everything? Or do you throw away ideas, thought, inscription along the road, guide from the tutor or advice from parent? The amount of information you receive makes you genius. Be teachable. Develop habit of thinking over all ideas before you trash them. They may add to your power as student. Gray matter refers to the darker tissue of the brain and spinal cord; literally waiting to receive axons. The amount of this tissue means that communication happens more quickly and effectively. This is scientific in nature.

The approach of genius is different from other people. Consider how you approach a particular problem. Perhaps you start with a flood of ideas. Then, most likely you start to eliminate these ideas. One won't work because you don't have money. Another won't work because you tried it before and failed. Yet another possibly will not work because no one will be on board with it, so slowly but surely, you impede each of your ideas and come out with one or two that might work. The genius brain works differently. Ideas are not eliminated based on efficacy or practicality. Everything is considered.[xcii] Thoughts are not immediately disqualified. A genius often tries many different avenues to arrive at a desired result, rather than simply deciding which ones will work and which ones won't.

Another trait that was identified by Nancy Andreason, the first female tenure-tracked English professor at the University of Iowa and a leading neuroscientist,[xciii] is that the creative people (geniuses) like to teach themselves rather than be taught by others. Think of the creative geniuses who were high school drop-outs – Bill Gates, Steve Jobs, and Mark Zuckerberg. "Because their thinking is different, my subjects often express the idea that standard ways of learning and teaching are not always helpful and may even be distracting, and that they prefer to learn on their own,"[xciv] she writes. Does it mean you should not complete your education? No! Some genius used to suffer exuberance and curiosity. You are privilege than them. You need to discover facts on your own and still source from others: teachers, parent, colleagues, instructors, etc.

Creative people persist against disbelief and rejection. When you're coming up with new unheard-of ideas, you're pushing against the status quo. Rejection and disbelief are inevitable. It's what you do in the face of those that matters most. New idea attracts new enemy. Andreasen found that creative geniuses are strong when presented with such disbelief. "They have to confront doubt and rejection," she writes. "And yet they have to persist in spite of that, because they believe strongly in the value of what they do." Nobody wants you to think above the culture, tradition, normal life or instructions. If you do, there will be rejection and envy. This is applicable to preceding geniuses but you must not quit. If you feel bad and accept rejection persistently, it might breed emotional pain, which can manifest as depression or anxiety. However, after the rejection, your new idea will create atmosphere of acceptance because everyone will benefit from your knowledge.

Now that you know you have ability to solve problems, let's examine the power of student's mind.

Power of creation

"What another would have done as well as you, do not do it. What another would have said as well as you, do not say it. What another would have written as well, do not write it. Be faithful to that which exists nowhere but in yourself—and thus make yourself indispensable." —Andre Gide[xcv][xcvi]

Creativity is the first power God put in the mind of man. Yet many people wonder if they have any creative abilities at all. Have you one time looked around you and appreciate the good state of art man's creativity has done? And this is just the beginning. Creativity is the greatest gift of human intelligence. The more complex the world becomes, the more creative we need to be to meet its challenges. [xcvii] As we grow, knowledge grows even faster than age. It will come to a time when African graduates will not get white collar job until he/she is able to design and develop creative and feasible ideas that will boost CV? Your certificate may not grade your true creative power until you do something. Some parents do not know their children worth because the children have never displayed creativity. Robert W. Weisberg, a psychologist, in his book, *Creativity: Understanding Innovation in*

Problem Solving, Science, Invention, and the Arts,[xcviii] comments on the demand for creativity in the society. He said, "Creative thinking is big business. Our largest and most prestigious corporations, as well as the largest government agencies, are constantly searching for ways to be more innovative, and they pay handsome fees to consultants who will help them achieve new levels of innovation from their employees. Institutions of higher education also take interest in teaching creative thinking. Many university business schools offer courses that are designed to provide business leaders—both those of the future and present-day ones who return for a refresher—with skills that will enable them to solve on-the-job problems." This may be the next level in our education around African countries.

How to Be Creative as a Student

Accept yourself as God calls you – "You are wonderfully and fearfully made."[xcix] Believe that all things are possible. Discover the problem. Do not be intimidated by the weight of the problem. Analyze your views. Research for likely problems with their solutions. Gather your thought together. Have time to think over each idea. Always test-run your ideas. Keep learning – you need to build on some people's foundation. At the end something new will show forth. Create conducive environment for yourself; for creativity and innovation are enabled by environments that engage with diversity, celebrate complexity, and value collaboration. Know that creativity is individual, collective, developing, and interpersonal; it stems from internal and external sources of inspiration and is motivated as you read and learn.

Power of invention

Where there is chaos, problem and lack, invention grows. Problems give birth to invention. "Inventing it must be humbly admitted, does not consist in creating out of bid but of chaos", Mary Shelley.[c] Yes! People from every corner of the world, of different ages, with different levels of education invent by identifying problems, pursuing ideas, and developing new solutions. The key to inventing is identifying a need and devising an original solution. Maybe a better question is, "Is there anyone who is not an inventor?" Everyone has the capacity for invention. We all solve problems through inventive thinking. In Nigeria, we have dynamic inventors, such as: **Emmanuel Okekunle,**[ci] a 22-year-old senior secondary school graduate and an aspiring inventor who says Nigerian youths could do more if the Government provided adequate support. He graduated from Cherubim and Seraphim College, Jos, Plateau State, in 2010. At the age of 5, he became interested in designing and constructing things and he constructed a wheelbarrow to help him carry up to five litres of water. At 7, he started developing electric toy cars using motors, batteries and tomato tins. In JSS1, he designed a toy helicopter. In SS2, he was encouraged by a teacher who told his students their inventions could secure them a scholarship, he constructed a rechargeable lamp, fan, emergency alarm, electric waste bin that converts waste to ashes, and an aquarium, among other things; **Jelani Aliyu**[cii] is the creative mind behind the Chevrolet Volt car. Aliyu comes from Sokoto State of Northern Nigeria working as the Senior Creative Designer of the US General Motors. He is the man who designed the Chevrolet Volt which has become one of the most admired American cars globally; Nigeria's **Saheed Adepoju**[ciii] is a young man with big dreams. He is the inventor of the Inye, a tablet computer designed for the African market; **Seyi Oyesola**[civ] is credited with the co-invention of CompactOR or the "Hospital in a Box", a solar-powered life-saving operating room which can be transported to remote areas of Africa and set up within minutes; **Dr. Otu Oviemo Ovadje**[cv] is a Nigerian medical Doctor who is credited with the invention of the Emergency Auto Transfusion System (EAT-SET), which is an effective, low-cost and affordable blood auto-transfusion mechanism that saves patients in developing countries. He has patented the invention in nine (9) countries. The EAT-SET system recovers blood from the patient's internal bleeding organs. This device has the ability of using the patient's own blood and in a safe manner re-infuses it into the patient's blood system. And who is the next inventor? It should be you. Your mind can also conceive these great discoveries and inventions. It starts from the mind to the field of action with knowledge derived from your reading and learning. At this point, I need to educate you more on invention and its rudiments.

Exploration is the engine that drives innovation. Innovation drives economic growth. So let's all go exploring – Edith Widder

What's an invention?

An invention is a useful creation that didn't exist before. An invention usually fills a need or solves a problem. Inventions often make the world a better place. Inventions can be things (e.g., a cell phone or wheelbarrow) as well as ideas (e.g., a new method for tying a knot, or a story). An invention often makes something better (e.g., faster, stronger, cheaper, easier, safer or more efficient, attractive, useful, accurate, fun, or productive). But as long as it's a new way to do something, it's still invention even if it isn't necessarily better than what existed before.[cvi]

Invention might look so crazy at first but years will appreciate the effort when innovation grows on its soil – Allen Olatunde

Why do we invent?

Inventing is a process. It starts with a need and ends up with something new—the actual invention.[cvii]

1.   **To solve problems:** Inventors are skilled at spotting ways to improve a situation or process. The discussion in this book help students develop solutions to problems by seeing themselves as potential inventors of new things or ideas. We live in and among problems and it has become or way of life. My reader, wake up and develop something better to solve African problems.

2.   **To improve our world**: Imagine how different our lives would be without inventions, such as computers, refrigerators, car, electricity, generator, plastic, and medicine. Inventions improve things at home, at school, in the community, and in the world. Your generation is waiting for you.

3.   **To enjoy the creative process**: Invention involves both thinking and doing. I write this book to get students

involve in the process of thinking about a problem and then doing something about it.

Process of Inventing

Identify a problem and/or realizing that something can be improved. Talk to people who might use the invention. Brainstorm creative solutions to a problem. Devise and test the solutions (i.e., experimenting). Apply science and engineering concepts. Use tools, materials, and techniques to make workable solutions. Try again when things don't work out. You can "Fail fast" and "Succeed sooner!" You must see a project through by being motivated, persistent, and dedicated. Inventors' and engineers' initial ideas rarely solve a problem. Instead, they try different ideas, learn from mistakes, and try again. The series of steps they use to arrive at a solution is called the design process.[cviii] Do something today.

Few quotes about creativity and innovation that may inspire your mind for action[cix]

1. "The creative is the place where no one else has ever been. You have to leave the city of your comfort and go into the wilderness of your intuition. What you'll discover will be wonderful. What you'll discover is yourself." — Alan Alda

2. "It is better to have enough ideas for some of them to be wrong, than to be always right by having no ideas at all." — Edward de Bono

3. "Genius means little more than the faculty of perceiving in an unhabitual way." — William James

4. "The creative person wants to be a know-it-all. He wants to know about all kinds of things ancient history, nineteenth century mathematics, current manufacturing techniques, hog futures. Because he never knows when these ideas might come together to form a new idea. It may happen six minutes later, or six months, or six years. But he has faith that it will happen." — Carl Ally

5.   "Creativity is inventing, experimenting, growing, taking risks, breaking rules, making mistakes, and having fun." — Mary Lou Cook

6.   "You can't wait for inspiration; you have to go after it with a club." — Jack London

7.   "Every artist dips his brush in his own soul, and paints his own nature into his pictures." — Henry Ward Beecher

8.   "The world is but a canvas to the imagination." — Henry David Thoreau

9.   "Creativity is… seeing something that doesn't exist already. You need to find out how you can bring it into being…" — Michele Shea

10.   "The most potent muse of all is our own inner child."– Stephen Nachmanovitch

11.   "Everyone who's ever taken a shower has had an idea. It's the person who gets out of the shower, dries off and does something about it who makes a difference." — Nolan Bushnell

12.   "All great deeds and all great thoughts have a ridiculous beginning." — Albert Camus

13.   "You write your first draft with your heart and you re-write with your head. The first key to writing is to write, not to think." — Sean Connery

14.   "Ideas are like rabbits. You get a couple and learn how to handle them, and pretty soon you have a dozen." — John Steinbeck

15.   "If you hear a voice within you say, 'You cannot paint,' then by all means paint, and that voice will be silenced." — Vincent van Gogh

16.   "Where observation is concerned, chance favours the prepared mind." – Louis Pasteur

17.   "I shall become a master in this art only after a great deal of practice." — Erich Fromm

18.   "Creativity is contagious. Pass it on." — Albert Einstein

19. "The principle goal of education is to create men who are capable of doing new things, not simply of repeating what other generations have done – men who are creative, inventive and discoverers." — Jean Piaget

20. "An invasion of armies can be resisted, but not an idea whose time has come." — Victor Hugo

21. "An idea that is developed and put into action is more important than an idea that exists only as an idea." — Edward de Bono

22. "Conditions for creativity are to be puzzled; to concentrate; to accept conflict and tension; to be born every day; to feel a sense of self." — Erich Fromm

23. "Every day is an opportunity to be creative – the canvas is your mind, the brushes and colours are your thoughts and feelings, the panorama is your story, the complete picture is a work of art called, 'my life'. Be careful what you put on the canvas of your mind today – it matters." — Innerspace

24. "I can't understand why people are frightened of new ideas. I'm frightened of the old ones." John Cage

25. "To live a creative life, we must lose our fear of being wrong." — Joseph Chilton Pierce Quotes

26. "You can't use up creativity. The more you use, the more you have." — Maya Angelou

27. "A man may die, nations may rise and fall, but an idea lives on." — John F. Kennedy

28. "Do not fear to be eccentric in opinion, for every opinion now accepted was once eccentric." — Bertrand Russell

29. "Life is trying things to see if they work." – Ray Bradbury

30. "The stone age didn't end because they ran out of stones." – unknown

Power of research

When last have you deliberately visit a place or person to know more about something you did not know? The more you desire to know the more your energy to seek for knowledge. "You write your first draft with your heart and you re-write with your head. The first key to writing is to write, not to think", says, Sean Connery.[cx] This makes me also to coin this statement, "Read a book, don't think about a book." Reading builds up a demand to research what someone first did. The power of research is in the mind and the mind has power to engage your five senses into action. Any research work that keeps abode only in the mind is as useless as gas flare in Nigeria.[cxi] What you need is your body and mind to move out for resources and knowledge. Power of research is conceived with sure possibility. In research, you can get anything out of its shell. However, not all research works are without failure. Michael Faraday failed many times before, he got it right. Failure is a true test of your endurance in research. When you fail, you know another way that does not work. You will not follow such path again because you failed there. A failure is not an end but a means to successful end. When you fail, do you discover why you fail? If you do, you have done a research.

Power of research has ability to draw needed materials for the task. When you need food to eat, your mind thinks fast on how to get to market, buy raw food, fill gasoline, ignite stove, provide water, pot, matches, plates and spoon. All these will locate themselves to you because you need them. I know you also will engage your sense to get them fast. So also the attempt to solve human problem with your career. A process of research needs time, concentration and available resources (men, money, method, medium and materials). Research gives us opportunity to resurrect what others bury unused. The Stone Age discovered what was needed and left others for whoever wants more. "The Stone Age didn't end because they ran out of stones." – Unknown.[cxii] Yes! They used all for themselves. It is left for us to re-invent the hidden stone ideas for our present use. You can see and search for what other generations have not been able to discover through research. Reading is just a secret exposer. Every author writes to keep the secret in a book, but student with mind for learning and research will expose the secret. My dear reader, please endeavor to read wide for research is the mother of discovery. I will share with you some people who got prospered because they engaged their mind with enough reading.

I heard about a man (through oral tradition) that read his Bible for the purpose of research. He got to the story of Moses in the Bible when the mother made colt for him with papyrus leaves. This creativity touched him. He started research on the leaf of papyrus and later discovered that wherever this plant grows there is possibility of crude oil dam underneath.[cxiii] He was mad at the research and ran to the government for further research and exploration. They signed Memorandum of Understanding (MOU) with agreement of certain percentage if the research is feasible economically for the nation. The team of engineers explored the land and saw untouched dam of crude oil. This research made this man a wealthy person for life.

Another story comes from a retired world renowned Neurosurgeon, Doctor Benjamin Carson. He was raised by a single mother. One day, his mother, Mrs. Carson saw Benjamin's failing grades; she determined to turn her sons' lives around. She sharply limited the boys' television watching and refused to let them outside to play until they had finished their homework each day. She required them to read two library books a week and to give her written reports on their reading even though, with her own poor education, she could barely read what they had written. Within a few weeks, Carson astonished his classmates by identifying rock samples his teacher had brought to class (that is the effect of further reading called research). He recognized them from one of the books he had read. "It was at that moment that I realized I wasn't stupid," he recalled later. Carson continued to amaze his classmates with his newfound knowledge and within a year he was at the top of his class.[cxiv]

If you are planting for a year, sow rice; if you are planting for a decade, plant trees; if you are planning for lifetime, educate people – Chinese Proverb

Research grows with age. In AD 105, Paper was first made in China. According to tradition, Ts'ai Lun, a eunuch attached to the court of the Chinese emperor Ho Ti, makes the first paper. He probably used mulberry bark, making the paper on a mold of bamboo strips.[cxv] This is great. Can you see what paper has done for the world today? The paper when it was first discovered would not be too good, neat, simple and light as we have it today. It is still the power of research in some students' mind that simplifies its state for convenience. Research is continuous. As you discover a solution, the solution itself will give birth to another problem. The antidote of this problem is continuous research. As student, you are endowed with power of research to know how and why, try to explore it.

I had privilege to observe the decadence of 'copy and paste' syndrome in higher institutions when the time of long essay comes. The project work supposed to show your ability to reason, discover a problem and proffer solution. It is a pity that many students collect previously used projects from friends and re-present to the lecturers for approval. This is academic theft and forgery. Most students cannot write ordinary term papers, talk less of thesis/dissertation. The problem is from the class – research and methodology class. Other problems are from the lazy students, poor library setup, time frame, inability to explore the minds, and lastly, they never see problem as they learn. The years at school should expose you to series of societal, communal or global problems which your course should be able to proffer solution. What you study is your discipline because you give up right and privilege only to pass through rigorous learning. Your discipline approves you as professional problem solver on your field. It is a pity that most African graduates are not marketable again because of inability to research, reason and formulate solution. Will you be one of them? You have the capacity to be distinctive and different student. Explore your mind. Engage your senses. Explore the world.

CHAPTER FIVE
WORLD FOR THE STUDENT'S MIND

The external world has great effect on your internal world. What you see, feel, touch, hear or smell has effects on your thought as students. Human senses connect mind to the outside world. Quiet environment is an intellectual blessing for learning. You know that. Every learner wants to be in his/her world of assimilation before starting to read. Even if you are in your world and the world is not managed, arranged or under-resourceful, it is equal to none. When you sleep to dream, you dream under an encouraging atmosphere suitable for sleep. If not, you will be disturbed. So also the student with great burden to solve societal problem must have his/her our world for learning. Learning begins with five senses–the gateway to the mind. What they perceive will send signal to the mind whether the environment is conducive or not. Eye likes attractive and lovely place; ears wants noiseless atmosphere; nose also desires good and non-offensive environment, etc. The picture of good learning environment comes first from the mind, i.e. the way you want your room to be for studying. This will actually create passion and determination for reading/studying. Some classes, libraries and study rooms put off students because they are not attractive and comely for learning.

To setup an environment that your mind will stay long to read, you must consider the purpose of learning (why you want to read–for examination, test, interviews, leisure or personal edification); duration of learning (for how long–2 hours, 5 hours, all night reading, or full day studying); and the process of learning (how to go about the learning–library research, close door reading, outdoor observation, public reading with groups, etc.) All these must be considered to setup learning atmosphere. In this chapter, I shall expose you to different worlds for learning and some guiding tips to stay long and be innovative.

A child educated only at school is an uneducated child – George Santayana

Study room tips[cxvi]

Find a good desk (or table) and chair.

You want to be comfortable, but not so comfortable that you lose focus or fall asleep. (Your bed is not the greatest option for assignment, it turns out.) It makes your mind rest. You also need adequate workspace to spread out. Find a desk or table with a top that rests somewhere between your waist and rib-cage when you sit at it, so that your elbows can rest easily upon it without having to hunch your shoulders forward. You also want to be able to rest your feet flat on the ground. Use a comfortable chair that fits the height of the desk / table.

Ensure adequate lighting.

A study area that is too dark will not only make it easier to nod off, it can exacerbate eye strain, which will put a damper on any study session. It's almost impossible to stay focused on your studies while straining your eyes to read in dim lighting, or squinting and getting a headache under harsh artificial lights. Harsh lighting, such as fluorescent light, can be bad for your eyes too. Use a desk lamp to focus light on your workspace, and also a nearby table or overhead light to brighten the area. If natural light is available, certainly make use of it. Be aware, though, that while the natural light provided by a window can be refreshing and calming, the temptation to stare out the window may hamper your studying. Just be sure that the activity—passersby, traffic, your neighbor's lively pet—is not going to distract you.

Gather your supplies.

Make sure you have all the materials you need for studying close at hand, so you don't waste time fumbling around for a ruler or pen. Keep usual school supplies like pens or pencils, erasers, paper, jotters, and so on in assigned areas on the desk or in a handy drawer. Keep a traditional pocket dictionary and calculator nearby, even though your phone can probably do the jobs of all two. Using your phone to do calculation or spell-check is an open invitation to distraction by the million other things you can do on it.

Consider a clock.

This depends on the type of person you are. Will a clock motivate you to keep studying for an hour more, or remind you that your favourite TV show is on in only 15 minutes (or make you think "I've only been studying for that long?!")? Try using a clock to set time-related study goals. You can also use the clock or timer feature on your phone or a watch to help you do this. Decide to study in an amount of time, such as 30 minutes. Don't allow yourself any distractions for that period of time. When it's up, take a little break to reward yourself! You could also try out a timer for even more precise time-keeping, especially if you are preparing for a timed exam like the CBT-UTME, SAT or school based exam.

Detach from your phone.

It is hard to ignore the enticement of your phone when studying. The modern smartphone is perhaps the ultimate tool and the ultimate distractor. Put it away when you study, or you may find yourself browsing Facebook, Whatsapp or texting a friend without even realizing you'd picked up the phone. Shut your phone off or put it in silent mode so the temptation of notification doesn't drag you away from your studies. Also try placing it well out of reach so you can't reflexively grab for it. If you are using your phone as a calculator or other tool, consider putting it in "airplane mode," which shuts off wireless connections. You can turn them back on for your (brief) study breaks.

Block out distracting sounds.

Some people do well with background noises that are distinct enough to be distracting. Others need total silence to work. Figure out what works well for you, and plan your space accordingly. Focus your study time on studying, and save things like TV and music for leisure time. If you prefer music, try light classical or at least something without lyrics. You want something that negates audio distractions without becoming one itself. Don't use headphones if you have a choice. They seem to hinder focus and information retention for many people, probably because the sound does not as easily blend into the background. Once you know how your brain handles noise, pick study locations that match your sound profile.

Use the space only for studying.
If your study space is your bed, you'll be more tempted to think of (or actually) sleep. If it is where you play computer games, gaming; the dining room table, eating; and so on. You will be more likely to create distracting learning environment. If it is possible for you to carve out a space - even a corner, a large closet, etc. - dedicated exclusively to studying, do it. Associate your presence there only with studying. It is your mindset that works. If this is not an option, do what you can to transform the multipurpose space into study space. Clear away food, dishes, centerpieces, etc., from the dining room table.

Avoid eating while studying.
Try to avoid over-consuming sugar and caffeine/coffee while studying. These can make you feel nervous and lead to "crashes" later. Try saving your snack for when you take a study break. You'll be more aware of what you're eating, and it's a nice way to reward yourself for a job well done. Don't ignore your body's needs, though. Set yourself a meal or snack break, or give yourself a specific amount of time before you replenish your tea. This way, you take care of your mind and your body.

Make it yours.
Try to locate your study space in an area that suits you. If you need dead silence, find a tucked away corner, a basement, a spare bedroom, whatever you can find. Go ahead and make a "Do Not Disturb," "Quiet, please," or "Hey, knock it off -- I'm studying here!" sign to post, depending on your personality. Adorning your study space with posters, signs, and photos that are important to you may help give you that morale to keep going. Just make sure they don't become distractions rather than motivators. Figure out

what kind of motivation works for you. A poster of the car you hope to get after you pass these exams and graduate. Copies of your earlier exams in chemistry with poor scores that you are determined to improve upon. Determine whether you need more of a "push" or a "pull" (or a carrot or stick, if you prefer) to keep you motivated.[cxvii]

Consider the temperature and humidity

For a short time, you may be able to stay focused in hot or humid places, but after a while, these circumstances can become unbearable. Similarly, if you're too cold, that quickly becomes all you can think about, and studying suffers. When you can control your environment—you have access to a thermostat, for example—set the temperature to a comfortable, constant level. But if you have to study at a library or public place where you can't control the temperature, try to have a sweater or glass of ice water handy.

Library usage
Get to know your library

The resources available to you will vary a lot depending on whether you're using an academic library at a large university, polytechnic, secondary, a public library in a large or small community. Find out early what resources your library has, by visiting and taking a tour with the library attendant, if possible. Some college libraries offer an online tour of the library or a self-guided tour using handouts in addition to tours guided by librarians. Libraries build their collections based on what they think their clients will need, so the collections of reference materials, fiction and non-fiction will differ between a public and an academic library. Be aware of what kind of collection you're working with, and make arrangements to visit a different library if necessary.

Learn to browse - understand the classification scheme in your library. A library's classification scheme is a system by which books are organized to be placed on the shelves. Browsing the shelves is an important step when you're trying to get ideas for your research project, reading, assignment or invention, so it's worth the effort to become familiar with your library's system. In a smaller library, many times you can bypass the catalog as a starting point and go directly to the shelves for a first look at your topic, so long as you have a chart of the classification scheme as a guide.

Learn how library catalogs work

A library catalog is a listing of all the items held by a particular library. A cataloguer examines the item (book, video, map, audio tape, CD, etc.) and decides how it will be described in the library's catalog and under what subject it will be classified. When the item is entered into the library's catalog database, information is entered into different fields, which are then searchable by users. The library catalog will tell you if the library keeps a particular periodical in its collection, but will not list all the articles within the periodical, nor will it necessarily even list all the issues of the periodical which are kept.

Consult the reference librarian for advice

Reference librarians can help save you a lot of time because they know their library's collection very well—both the reference collection and the nonfiction collection—and can often tell you "off the top of their heads" whether or not the library has a particular item you're looking for.[cxviii] They are also skilled searchers, both of the library's catalog and of online resources such as CD-ROM, online databases and the internet. In addition, they're trained in teaching others to use these resources and are glad to do so. As written by Kathryn L. Schwart of The iSchool at Drexel, College of Information Science and Technology, with major support from the College of Information at Florida State University.

Rules in the library

Whenever you visit a library, you don't bring in textbook that is not registered by the librarian and you don't take away book without the consent of the librarian. You do not tear any page of a book because you need the page. You do not eat or drink inside the library. Some books are poisoned to preserve their strength for years. You need to wash your hand after library usage. When you study in the library, you need to jot down you discoveries, points and findings for further work. Avoid noise, music, or chatting with other friends. You mind your business in the library. Let your mind be at rest whenever you get a sit and your books. Be focused and proactive to learn. Do not ignore any facts, it may add to your learning. When you discover any difficulty, consult the librarian for help. If you see any interesting or useful books that you cannot read all, you can borrow. Make sure you follow the due process of borrowing. Let your mind be conscious of the environment. Forget your worries, fear, or difficulties. Plan your next visit with your librarian.

Internet resources exploration tips

Internet has been the relatively close source of information to anyone in the world. We surf net to get data and information for our work, project and assignments. How useful, reliable and truthful are the information? Since anyone can publish on the internet, students should ensure that the information they are sourcing for assignments is accurate and reliable.[cxix] This chapter provides a starting point for internet resources evaluation and how to avoid internet plagiarism. There are four questions to ask when evaluating internet resources.[cxx] They are: What are the author's qualifications? What is the purpose and scope of the source? How accurate and reliable is the source? And how current is the source?

What are the author's qualifications?[cxxi]

- Is the author's name visible? Does the author have an affiliation with an organization or institution?
- Does the author list his or her credentials? Are they relevant to the information presented?
- Is there a mailing address or telephone number included, as well as an e-mail address?
- Be skeptical of any web page that does not identify an author or invites you to contact an unnamed "Webmaster."

What is the purpose and scope of the source?

- Does the page exhibit a particular point of view or bias? Is the site sponsored by a group or organization? If it is sponsored by a group or company, does the group advocate a certain philosophy? Try to find and read **"About Us"** or similar information.
- Does the site seek to publicize a product? If advertising appears on a web page, try to determine the extent to which it may be influencing informational content i.e. does the data seem manipulated to serve the ads (advertisement), or are the ads simply used to fund the site?
- The origination of the site can provide indications of the site's mission or purpose.[cxxii]

The most common domains are:[cxxiii]

- *org:* An advocacy web site, such as a not-for-profit organization.
- *com:* A business or commercial site.
- *net:* A site from a network organization or an Internet service provider.
- *edu :* A site affiliated with a higher education institution.
- *gov:* A federal government site. This may also include public schools and community colleges.

3. How accurate and reliable is the source?[cxxiv]

- Can factual information on the site be verified? There are no standards or controls on the accuracy of information available via the Internet. It is therefore up to you to determine how accurate information is. Determine whether the factual information on a website can be corroborated elsewhere – through a reference to or citation of a clearly reliable source, for example. If the text appears slanted to support any advertising, then you should not trust the reliability of facts on the site.

- How credible and authentic are the links to other resources? Are links to other sources evaluated or annotated in any way? If footnotes, bibliographies, and hypertext links are used, do they add authority, credibility, or depth to the argument or only seem to do so?

- What about Wikipedia? Wikipedia is a useful tool for gaining a general understanding of a topic and for providing some references. However, as its own disclaimer a state, information on Wikipedia is contributed by anyone who wants to post material. Some information on Wikipedia may well be accurate. However, because experts do not review the site's entries, it is not possible to know for certain. This may mean that information on Wikipedia is less reliable (and less up-to-date) than a regular, peer reviewed, encyclopedia.[cxxv]

4. How current is the source?

- It is important to make sure any internet source you use is current. Ask yourself, is there a creation date? Is the information up-to-date or are the resources outdated? Is there a date when the information was last revised? Do the links still work? If not, it may be an indication that the information has not been updated recently.

- Note this: age is relative on the web. A document that is three or four years old can still be "timely" in certain disciplines such as social science or arts and design. However, in fields where knowledge develops rapidly (e.g., the sciences) or data is expected to change (e.g., statistics), currency is more important.[cxxvi]

Internet usage guide:

As a student who wants to learn, be careful of what you want to do. Always go online with planned paper of what to do. Do not click any link that comes your way. It may be porn links that will surely soil your mind. Some links are for adverts (ads). Beware! You need to browse for data from useful sites such as Google, yahoo, etc. You can surf with list of topics, ideas or keywords that well explain your project, invention, etc. When you go online for surfing, you can save your page for offline reading, or surf for pdf files of the topics you are looking for. [cxxvii] This will allow you to create more time to study the information. Always keep record of your sites information to avoid plagiarism.

CHAPTER SIX
HOW TO PREPARE FOR EXAMINATIONS

All students learn, read and study to write examination. Studying for an examination should be more than just a cramming session; successful studying is an ongoing process that begins in the first day of classes and it involves managing your time and learning effectively. It also involves developing a foundation for pre-exam review. The exam supposed to show the intelligence of the students on paper. African educational system puts more effort on final exam than continuous assessment test. It is 70:30 ratios. That is why students read extensively and tirelessly for final exam. However, the strength of a student goes beyond the exam. As for you, do not read for examinations; read for life consumption. To pass examination, it starts from your mind perceptive. Some fail before they failed. Cowardice dies many times before his death. You need to believe in yourself, your reading and God. However, in my research I got some strategies to prepare and pass examinations from an online page (paraphrased).[cxxviii] It actually guides on examination preparations (the points were paraphrased for student's consumptions). This site outlines several tips and strategies that students can use to enhance their studying during university, secondary or primary school time.

Review material regularly
Before you can begin studying for an exam, good study habits begin much earlier in the term or semester. To effectively study, it is essential you review regularly the material from lectures, seminars and textbooks in a consistent fashion. Get into the habit of reviewing your notes daily. As eat daily so you must read your notes.

Reviewing your notes weekly

At the end of each week, go through your notes for all of your classes to ensure you understand the content. Rewrite any lecture/class notes if they are too muddled or disorganized. Organize your notes into binders or file folders. Ensure the notes are placed in sequence with other notes. Make summary notes on the important concepts and information. Look at how the material covered relates to the course as a whole. This is summary of reading. Make it your habit.

Identifying when you need help for long before the exam

Getting into the habit of asking questions, going to see the professor or class teacher or seeking out friends to help you understanding something that is difficult is wise action as student. Do this long before the examinations come closer, to avoid rush hour tutorial.

Identify examination essentials

Before you can conduct any meaningful studying, you must first define the scope of the exam. You need to determine what knowledge and skills are being evaluated. Gather as much information about the exam as you can. Although it's not appropriate to ask specifically what will be asked on the exam, there is nothing wrong with requesting or finding out the following:

- What does the course outline say about the exam and the focus of this course?
- How much is the exam worth in terms of a percentage of your final mark?
- Is this a required course you need to get into next class or higher institution?
- What mark would you like to get in this course? What results will you need on this particular test or exam to achieve that mark?
- Which lectures, readings, assignments and problems could be part of the exam?

- Is there a greater focus on the textbook, lectures or both?
- How much of the term or semester's content is covered by the exam (the whole term/semester or just before the Continuous Assessment Tests)?
- For problem-solving classes, will formulas be provided or do they need to be memorized. Can you take in your own formula sheet to the exam?
- Are there any materials you will need to bring to the exam (e.g., calculator)?
- Are the teachers or the professor going to give a review session before the examination?
- Is there a Supported Learning Group (tutorial class/group discussion) for this course?

How to organize & integrate resources

Previous tests - Be sure to review any previous tests you've had in the subject/course. Analyze errors you've made in the past, recognizing where you lost marks. Re-do the test or examination sincerely.

Making a study guide - A lot of students make study guides. Here is a brief overview of one method. Once you find out which lectures, readings and textbook pages will be covered by the exam, print out or gather up the related lecture and textbook notes. Organize these pages into piles, separated by topics. Label each of the piles with the corresponding topic title. Staple or paper-clip all papers in each pile together. Read through your notes and determine if they can be condensed (i.e. see what information is not needed or not covered by the exam).

Creating an outline - An outline can be thought of as a condensed study guide. Outlines attempt to condense large amounts of information you have from all your course sources into a logical system. Focus on broad subjects, key issues and concepts. You don't need to be completely textual. You can use acronyms to reduce points into few words. Don't spend too long on preparing an outline. It is just one study aid

Plan your time

When is the best time to study? Everyone is different - choose a time you are most awake. Students find the most effective time for studying to occur between when they wake up and when they eat dinner. Yet some students work very well late into the night. Choose a time that is quiet and when your brain is ready to learn. *Where should you study? (Chapter five explains this subtopic).* Most students work best in isolation. Find a number of isolated study spots on or off campus and rotate through these locations when you study. Seek out those study spots so that you have choices and can change venues to prevent procrastination or avoid distractions. Studying in the dorm room or at home on your bed often just doesn't work for everyone. *How long should you study?* Generally, no more than one hour at a time without a break. Your break needs to be only 5-10 minutes, but it's important that you take an intellectual breather during this period. Doing something completely different on your break (e.g., reading a newspaper article, sending a few SMS or chat) will help refresh your mind. Generally, 30-60 minutes is an appropriate learning period for studying before taking a break.

Study actively

Active studying means you have to be engaged with the content. Most students make the mistake of relying on passive review which involves reading and re-reading their notes and assignments. They assume the more times they read the content the more they will remember it. Make the extra effort to get it into your head! Review your material, explain it (without looking) in your own words and out loud (if possible) and then check to see if you are correct. If you can close your eyes and create an argument from scratch or stare at a blank sheet of paper and reproduce a solution without a mistake, then you have fully understood the concept. Attempt difficult questions and later check for solution. Do it again until you are confident of the formula, theory or principle.

Teach the subject to a classmate

When you have to teach and explain a concept to someone else, you are actively understanding and interacting with the content. Have your classmate ask you questions for further explanation. Construct a practice quiz for each chapter in your study guide. The more you teach others, the more you know best.

Study Groups

Studying with a group of your friends can be both a fun and rewarding study method. For effective studying, it is important that you choose your group members wisely and follow a few rules. Study groups should not be the sole method of study and they are not for everyone; not let one member of the group dominate. Meet no more than 2-3 times a week for no more than 60-90 minute periods. Establish responsibilities for each group member. Stay motivated and commit more time to study

Use Strategies to Help Reduce Forgetting

Test yourself as you study. Use: Acronyms (**MR NIGER D** - is an acronym for characteristics of living things – Movement, Respiration, Nutrition, Irritability, Growth, Excretion, Reproduction and Death). *Analogies* and *Keywords* linked can also be helpful as you study.

Instructions during examinations

Whenever you are to write examination, be yourself. Let your mind be at rest. Avoid last minutes reading; it may affect your previous reading. Close your ears to any last minutes rumour of the exam questions; it may confuse you. When you sit down to write exam, pray to God for His help. Read every bit of instructions before you start the exam. Do not communicate with anyone in the hall. Do not do collective examination; it is treacherous and aberrant to the school law. Do not borrow anything from your friends or lend anyone anything. Concentrate on the questions. Prioritize your interest on the questions. That is, answer the ones you know by order of understanding. Do not waste time to ruminate over difficult ones. Always write your name on your answer script before you forget. Do not rush to be the first in the class–rat race. Be calm after the exam to crosscheck your answers; if there is omission, you can complete it. After all, let your mind be peaceful that you have done the best you can and leave the rest for God in prayer as you submit and go out of the hall.

Post-Exam Strategies

Some students simply do not think about their exams again, other than to say, "I will do better next time." Try to make an effort to review your exams thoroughly; especially if you did not perform as well you had wanted to. You'll need to find out why you made mistakes so you can adjust your studying and exam-writing next time. If your teacher, lecturer or instructor do not return your midterms or exams script, you can request to see your script (in an ideal school setup), and ideally within a few days when marks are pasted or shared. You may not be able to take notes while reviewing your exam, but some instructors are usually very willing to let you read through it. In the school where I served as Chaplain, the teachers give the scripts to the students in order to discover simple errors during collation and to know the right answers for the purpose of the next examinations.

CHAPTER SEVEN
CAREER DEVELOPMENT

From cradle to grave, the most common act of man is choice making. We take decision every day for better livelihood. On normal circumstances, a human being has choice of what to eat, drink, associate with, read, watch or wear. The choice of career is one out of many decisions we ought to make as long as we live. It is a crossroad with many links but only one is relevant to one's life. This is the time when suggestions, discoveries, observations, pressure, divinity, spiritism and self-will will fight to win the stage of your choice. This issue of career is related to many other decisions of life like, marriage, choice of country or residential area to settle, choice of religion and faith and choice of lifestyle. However, career is the main connector to other decisions of life. If one misses it, others may not last as they ought to be. When a matter is crucial, then it needs good attention to get to the good side with minimal and bearable risks, for every decision has risk embedded.

Career choice begins from the first year on earth when future formation begins. The child with brighter future starts from the four corner of the house. Career is who you are and what you can still be able to do. Career relates with internal and external factors of life in order to dig and fit in to the societal environment. Career can be interchanged with profession. Career is an occupation undertaken for a significant period of a person's life and with opportunities for progress.[cxxix] Career lasts as long as physical, emotional and intellectual strength strive. It is what you will be known for, even after you are no more. It will become a legacy for another generation through the input in your career. Career can be renamed occupation, job vocation, employment line and profession. Career is an individual's journey through learning, work and other aspects of life and also it is divine. It involves God who knows the end from the beginning. Career also involves your parents, counselors and professionals. Career is your choice. Whether up the hill or down the valley, that's your life. That's yours. Choose it. Enjoy it. Celebrate it.

In a gentle way, you can shake the world – Mahama Gandhi

Why choosing career?[cxxx]

Career and choice are inseparable twins. Career that is imposed is no more a career. It becomes a task from task-master. You must love and cherish what you will choose as career. Parents sometimes choose for children because of prestige attached to some career, especially medicine and law. There are thousands of careers to choose. A young student has the right to choose career under a flexible guidance of counselors, parents and professionals. Why do you need to choose your career?

If you do not choose, others will choose for you:

Choice is personal. When choice becomes impersonal then there is imposition. We take decision daily for survival and anyone who fails to do the same will be left behind or be helped with decision without his/her consent. Your parent is waiting for your choice. Also, the school wants to know. You cannot sit on the fence on career matter. You must take the lead first before others can assist. If not, you will go for what they dream for you. There is a renowned musician in Nigerian who wanted to choose music as career but the parents said "No, it is Veterinary Medicine". If you do not prove yourself mature and competent to choose, anyone will choose your future as they think it should be. Be smart and be prepared to take the lead first.

There is problem to solve:

Every assignment has a problem to solve. So also every career has societal problems to solve. Mechanics solve car problems. Dentists solve tooth problems. Lawyers solve legal problems. Accountants solve tax and monetary problem. Have you ever asked yourself questions that x-ray your career? You are born to save your world and generation. God has qualified you to be a perfect solution to someone. Your choice of career should be able to solve difficult situations in your time. This is the issue of life-purpose. You need to choose a career that will gladden your heart when unfortunate lives are saved, society is restructured and generations call you blessed. Today in our world, we keep celebrating Dr. Benjamin Carson, Neurosurgeon doctor, who detached and restored life to conjoined twins. We are waiting to celebrate someone again. I know it is you. Do not choose because your friend likes the career. We live to solve diverse problems. Choose yours now.

To avoid confusion:

Fusion of two things that are not compatible is called confusion. Confusion is not good for a future-minded student like you. Sometimes, our minds tell us we can do this, we can do that. Yet there is only one that you are born to do. When you are confused, do not choose in rash, rush or in haste. Consult your parents, counselors or professionals on careers. Be sure of your choice before developing yourself on career. Note this: it is painful to invest all strength and might in an assignment and one later discovers that it is a wrong one. The strength consumed already cannot be retrieved. It is hurting. Avoid futuristic confusion.

Human is insatiable:

In the study of human beings, the economists and psychologists agree that we are insatiable – no one can satisfy human beings. We have short span of interest on many things. Choose your career with keen interest of long term span. You can.

Personality goes with a specific career:

God is a perfect God. He created us with uniqueness that will help in choosing and developing career. Personality traits/skills are inborn and natural without pressure of duress. Some are introverts, extroverts, extremists, friendly, analytical, calculative, caring, reserved, observant, problem solvers, questioners, etc. Know yourself and choose rightly.

To create diversity:

If everyone is a doctor, who will keep money for everyone in the bank. If everyone is an engineer, law court will be locked and right of others will be denied. There is need for diversity. Career development can be in the class of medicine, law, engineering, building, education, science and technology, aviation, military, journalism, accounting and banking, carpentry, transportation, trading, pastoring, administration, etc.

For self-actualization:
Self-actualization is the peak of Abraham Maslow theory of man's need. When all needs of life is met, and then man can think of actualizing purpose for living. Self-actualization starts now. You want to be a great administrator, lawyer, engineer, sailor, pilot, trader, teacher, doctor, and so on, then dream it, study hard, choose it, and endure the training.

Risk management:
Every career has risk attached. We choose a career that has manageable and minimal risk. Choose with help of seasoned counselors who know the 'in and out' of career you may want to choose. You need help, do not do it alone.

FIVE LEVELS OF CAREER CHOICE
Due process is the spine of development. Career has levels which they link with one another. Career survives on these levels. The absence of one of the levels will dent the growth and success of career development. Let's look into the levels one after the other: Academic level; Personality level; Parental support level; Tertiary-societal level; and Future level.

Academic level:
Career grows on the pedestal of good academic level. As a student, the academic performance in the school determines the choice and passion for a career. It all starts from the first day at school. The interest level for learning and reading contributes to career development. When a student has a personal and undiluted interest in reading and studying of his/her books without or less supervision of parents, guardians or teachers, such a child is not far from success. Academic performance takes the major step in choosing career. The mid-term tests and termly examinations in schools evaluate the academic capacity that commensurate a career you can do. Seek advice from your

subjects and class teacher. Be frank about their evaluation. The remarks will help you to sit tight if you will still pursue the career.

Personality level:

This is a step forward from school to you. Who you are cannot be adulterated overnight. Personality trait is exceptional. There are schools of thoughts on personality development. Some look at man with temperament principles, while others on perception and rationality. Personality trait has uniqueness by gender, genetic factor, environment, exposure, status, etc. Some are extroverts (they can express themselves freely in speech and action without considering external factors of crowd, intimidations, fear, gender, etc.) and introverts (they are reserved and calm, not always at ease to speak for or being spoken for). Understand yourself to choose career. If an introvert student chooses law as a career, he/she may find it difficult to withstand intimidation, crowd, embarrassment, loss or inconvenience. That doesn't say introvert cannot study law. However, such a person would have discovered him/herself earlier and try hard to adjust to the demands of the career. Nevertheless, the personality trait does a great work in growing career. It is in you. To become a successful and bold lawyer, a 21st-century software developer, an actuarial scientist, a renowned neurosurgeon and so on, it all starts with you. You can stir up good features in you through good exposure, reading, practical actions, and mentoring. If you want to know and improve yourself, be simple and be approachable for correction.

Parental-support level:

Having good academic performance and the best personality trait without support, career development may be slow, can scatter or die naturally if support is nowhere to be found. Every student has support advantage of parents from cradle till youthful and useful age. This support level must be understood before choosing a career. If you choose a career that your parents reject, support roles will not be there. When you want to choose a career, know your parents/guardians minds. Know their worth and what they can afford annually. Let them know your choice before the time of rushing comes, so that they can prepare adequately for your future.

Tertiary-societal level:

Nigeria is a blessed country with universities, polytechnics, monotechnics and colleges of education. The sector has structure for career development. However, not all tertiary institutions can really help your dream career. The schools differ in past glory, tuition, ownership, structures, lecturers, equipment, facilities, learning environment, leadership, social and economic life and location. Our schools are loaded with good and bad elements that can make or mar your career. It is left for you to choose where to go. Before you will conclude on choice of school, seek the approval of your parents and the thorough counsel from your school counselor.

Future level:

Career choice is measured by the end result in the future. There is peak in career when self-actualization or regret may set in. Your choice of today will determine the result of tomorrow. In Nigeria and beyond, some careers have been lucrative and selling in the labour market. If you choice a career because you love it without considering the economic returns, you will be frustrated later. What are the factors to consider before choosing career for futuristic success?

Societal trend and relevance - There is always a paradigm shift of interest in the society. People do prefer career because it is recognized. Whenever the relevance is dropped, everyone talk less about the career. *Demand in labour market* - Labour market is big and wide. Everyone in the market wants to sell and gain. When a career earns big, people will rush into it. Before in Nigeria, nursing was not lucrative but now the season of relevance has come and young ladies want to be nurses because the take-home is handsome. How lucrative a career was, is and will be must be considered before choosing one. *Solution provider for society* - Non-monetary value of career to society also matters in choosing one as a student. I said it earlier that you are born to solve problems. Problems wait in the future for wrong choice of career while the right choice goes along with solution. Your relevance in the career goes with solution to long waited problems in the society. *Diversification* - Diversification gives room for expansion. The choice of your career should be able to allow you to add other entrepreneurship opportunities. Think about it. You can diversify at Masters' Degree level to related and relevant fields. As a student of great career, watch the level you are and adjust yourself to fit in to other levels. Remember that a choice of career that has academic level plus personality level with the backing of parental support level in the tertiary-societal level will survive in the future level.

INDICATORS OF SUCCESSFUL CAREER CHOICE

Reading culture - There is one thing that everyone needs to possess to change himself, environment, choice, beliefs, value system and actions. This is knowledge. Knowledge is known as information. And information is formed by the numbers of data you get from reliable sources. Knowledge can be sourced for through learning. Learning can be achieved through habitual reading culture (More in chapter One).

Uniqueness:

What you know - knowledge. What you can do - ability. What you prefer most - choice. All make you. Everyone has preference based on personal interest and value. Your uniqueness must not be traded away in career choice. You can admire others but do not lose yours. The point of uniqueness starts when everyone applauds you for an activity. Your uniqueness can win or lose. It is not a total failure, that's your uniqueness. Whenever you make progress in what you know best, do not laugh but smile. Whenever you fail despite your effort do not cry but be frank. Sit down and research why you progress so that you can monitor and master the pace. Your failure also needs investigation to know the weak point to be strengthened. What others do and fail, you can do it and be successful. Do not compare yourself to lose taste of your uniqueness.

Parents' guide and response:

Success indicator on career choice still flips back home. You cannot become what you have not been in the house. Charity begins from home. Your parents/guardians are your natural coach, instructor and guide on matter of life. Career is life. Parent/guardians do not want their child/ward to venture into what can ruin their lives. Therefore, the advice is to deliberately seek counsel from them and wait for the response. Do not fight back on their response. Do not insult them. God sometimes uses parents for their children to stop a wrong move, to guide rightly or to kickoff progressively into success.

School views:

School community consists of the principal, vice principals, HOD, teachers, students and you. Everyone knows your academic and potential performance. Their contribution is an indicator for a successful career. The classroom in the school is a test-tube for your career. How do you respond to issues in the class? Do you strive to solve problems in the school and classroom? This is a point where people will begin to suspect your dream career as you relate, resolve and revitalize hope for coming generations. What does your school say about your career? Do you have good testimony in the community? If not, start now to build good foundation for your dream career through academic excellence, good relationship and attitude to solve problems in the school.

O level results:

Career development stands solely on your O level result. The ability to have at least five credits pass is an indicator of success in career. Some try the exam for more than three times until they have it, only because it is the pass into tertiary institutions. Do your best to have it in time to save your passion from dwindling due to pressure, shame, intimidation and lost opportunities of admission.

Physical health status:

Sky is not the limit for anyone whose health is intact. Physical status of a career people is an indicator of success. How do you care for your body? Do you eat anything or drink alcohol? I learnt recently about a medical student who was diagnosed for cancer at the mid of her training in university. Now, she would only care for health and careless about career. Your physical fitness goes along way with your health status that indicates success in dream career.

Endurance level:

How enduring are you in life? Nothing comes easily. Career development grows on the wings of tolerance, endurance, perseverance, emotional stamina and large heart. Through thorns and barbs, colourful flowers blossom. Start to develop hormone for endurance. There is no career without stress. They are manageable ones. Choose a career that you know you can endure the years of training without giving up on the way. A medical doctor goes through different stages of training in the school, at the hospital and in the classroom. He/she will be exposed to dangerous and risky situations, yet he/she must attempt and move on. Be wise.

Knowing what to avoid:

Success indicator in career has many things to do and also others to avoid. A student who dreams to choose career successfully will run away from these things: unnecessary friendship and ungodly peers; sleeping when you suppose to read; too much activities that do not add to your career pursuit; too much food, junks, sweets, etc.; passion for malpractice and mercenary during examinations; addiction to television show and season movies; unnecessary apprehension about your parent ordeal, divorce, debt, illness, etc.; and alcoholism and drug abuse

REQUIREMENTS FOR CAREER DEVELOPMENT

Your dream career will become a reality one day. God has given you all that is needed. You are the only obstacle that can stop the fulfillment. There are some steps you must take to get to the top - it is called the requirement.[cxxxi] It is a long term process. It takes number of years to get all. But your endurance level will guide and guard you to the top. Note this: career is built on wings of diverse effort you are able to put on. Career begins from the heart to the sky. If you can dream it, you can become through these requirements listed below:

Complete O' level results

Every career has their root from the nine subjects required for admission into tertiary institutions. Why? All these rudiments of courses are basically taught in your secondary school. All you shall do in the tertiary institutions is to build on the subjects and narrow down your knowledge to your career. Try all your best to get Ordinary level results complete to start the journey into career with good speed.

Understudying and internship

During the course of learning in the tertiary institutions, you will go out of the campus to gain knowledge beyond books. The practical aspect of your career is achieved during the understudying in industries, companies, hospitals, firms and corporations. It can be inform of SIWES, Industrial Training (IT), apprenticeship, housemanship (the state of learning as a junior doctor training in a hospital post), etc. It depends on your course of study.

Passing through all levels of tertiary institutions with good grades

The citadel of learning and development is the tertiary institution you choose to attend. Your grade/result will determine your career strength. If you go to College of Education, you will have these certificates – NCE, B.Ed., Masters in Education, Ph.D. For Polytechnic – ND, HND, PDGE, Masters, PhD and for University – B.Sc., B.Tech., B.A., M.Sc., MBA, Ph.D. You can reach the last degree (Ph.D.)

Voluntary service to the nation

Another requirement that one needs to build career and confidence is National Youth Service Corps (NYSC) scheme. It helps one to serve based on the course you study in the tertiary institution. It promotes acts of service, loyalty and competence. Do your best to study with good grade, graduate without carry over and you will be posted to serve and act your career under good trial.

Professional bodies and examinations

Career becomes professional when you are certified by a group of professionals who have gathered wealth of knowledge to be shared with next generation through examination, meetings, seminars and guidelines of operation in that career. Before you can be allowed to operate, you must pass their examinations and get licensed. They are ICAN, Nursing and Midwifery Association, NBA, CIBN, CIS, CIPM, NSE, NMA, etc.

On-job-training, seminars and workshops

Career is developed as you work and learn. Schooling does not stop when you have the tertiary institution's certificate. That one is just a foundation. You will go for training, seminars or workshop which the organization, company or corporation where you work with will send you, either locally or abroad. Start to dream your career beyond your country shore.

Other requirements are mentoring, self-discovery and creativity, teaching others, wide exposure and traveling, library research and development, and years of working experience. At the end of all these requirements, you are at the top of your career. That's self-actualization. Trust God and you will get there. Do your best. Read hard now and sky will be the beginning of your great career.

CHAPTER EIGHT
DISTRACTIONS OF THE MIND OF STUDENT

Mind has eyes to see, ears to hear, nose to smell and skin to feel. How? All these senses have connection to the mind. Whenever they feed the mind with wrong information, it becomes distraction to the mind. As student, your mind should always connect to learning for fulfilment. Enemy of fulfilment is distraction. Distraction is just fusions of two words–distance and attraction. All that you think is beneficial to you not close. They are far away with false images. Distraction has power to change mind, sight and focus to another thing entirely without a reason. Such things may look attractive at distance, just take a deep walk closer, you will discover it is not worth living for. Youth, exuberance and curiosity cohabit together because they are psychological friends that must be managed. Students in the school have many distractions that can cause a paradigm shift from studentship to fun. Many students have lost their dreams via distractions on the way to stardom. Victims of distractions had never forgiven themselves because they after realized what they ran after was just a mirage. Is it sex, music, fun, power, status or fashion? They are situated at every stage of life; you will surely get there and be satisfied. Why running after them now to lose the key to future? Only the wise students will shun distractions.

Mind has a big reservoir with very large space but definite in use. If you fill your mind with distractions at first, there will be no space for other useful things. Though the space is still there but not for other things than the initial deposit. The student who dreams to solve communal and global problems will never allow distractions to drain out power of his dream. In this chapter, I shall educate you on the major distractions in the school and how they dominate student's mind against the dream.

Distraction one – Sexual immorality

In campuses, secondary schools and youthful settings, sex immorality has great effect on the students. As adolescents, teenagers and young adult grow, the emotional strength grows together in order to have feeling for one another. This emotion has made some students to grow wide and commit sexual immorality around the school corner. It is not news to talk about sex and its scandal in our schools because everyone gets involved in one way or the other - the students, the staff and the visitors to the school. In fact, sexual immorality is redefined by some students as fun and rights of expression. It is practiced in different forms in the school such as masturbation, lesbianism, nudity, pornography, rape, cohabitation, prostitution, payback, and modeling.

According to Microsoft Encarta 2009, masturbation[cxxxii] is practiced from secondary school level by the age range. During this period, more children gain experience with masturbation (self-stimulation of genitals). Surveys indicate that about one-third of all girls and about half of all boys have masturbated to orgasm by the time they reach the age of 13, boys generally starting earlier than girls. Because preadolescents tend to play with others of their own sex, it is not at all uncommon that early sexual exploration and experience may happen with other members of the same sex. This act has the way it endangers your mind if you are involved. It becomes addiction. It does not stop easily once starts. It has power to dominate you mind once the urge comes. It makes you secretive and lonely. You will be looking for dark corner or empty room to masturbate. This menace makes some boys to segregate themselves from girls because they have passion for individual sex orgasms. A mind who thinks sex will never concentrate during reading. Pictures, posters, novels, books, or movies with opposite sex or nude will surely prompt such person to look for secret place to act. Masturbation enslaves its victim. If you are enslaved with masturbation, you first need God. You need dissatisfaction with the status quo. You need to develop replacement mechanism for the evil. And you need to talk to someone about it now.

Lesbianism is common to female gender. It is very common to female hostels in the school. Whenever ladies of life-passion inhabit, the tendency to stir themselves for sex used to come up. It is a branch of homosexuality - sexual orientation toward people of the same sex. Female homosexuals are frequently called lesbians. Homosexuality appears in virtually all social contexts—within different community settings, socioeconomic levels, and ethnic and religious groups. The mind is at war whenever lesbianism prevails. Do not sell yourself to big girls of the campus. The health hazard is paramount. The mind can never think right if this evil resides there. God hates this evil. Africa culture is not also in support. Stand against whoever that wants to lure you into it. It ruins future: academic pursuit, marital satisfaction, societal right, etc.

Pornography[cxxxiii] is an act of viewing nude pictures and sex acts. It is everywhere in the school: on phones, as posters in the hostels/rooms/streets, on bill board along the road, on TV show and magazines. Students are the victim of this evil. The more you view the pictures the more you lose your mind to sex. The rape is born as the result of pornography and nudity. All these acts kill our mind. The dreams of leading the country, curing the sick ones, defending the innocent, building the nations are dying on the lap of *'Delilahs'*[cxxxiv] every day. Why do you enjoy what will not last? Students can be victim of sexual immorality through night partying, bad peer group, drunkenness, nudity, cohabitation, wrong mindset about sex, drug addiction, smoking, 'boy-girl-friendism', bad novels on romance, blue films and devilish magazine with nude models.

You can conquer this evil, if you can make a covenant with your eye and body that no evil will enter through. Avoid a bad group that does not believe in your values and dreams. Avoid romantic books. Do not give lustful thought a second reviews in your mind. Speak to Christian friends about your challenges. Be cautious in your relationships with opposite sex. Determine to wait till your wedding night. Always sanctify your mind with God's word. Pray always against temptations and evil desires. Believe God for victory. Replace your desire with positive acts. Give less attention to your lustful body. Retable your life purpose continuously. Do not be deceived with alternative to sex: using of condom, kissing and caressing, sex talk and jokes, etc. Set life target with deadlines – your mind will be occupied. Attend fellowship of believers with pure mind. Avoid too much of privacy. Sometimes, think of end: death and rapture. Ready to change location faster before lust hooks you down.

If you refuse all this advice, there are effects and consequence for sexual immorality. They are abortion, sexually transmitted diseases (STD), societal stigma, unwanted pregnancy and regrets, suspension and withdrawal from school due to academic retardation, early motherhood, future problems, barrenness, addicted to contraceptive pills, marital dissatisfaction, joblessness, inability to achieve future dream and others. I will like to share this story with you about a student who had sexual intercourse to her deadly regret.[cxxxv]

"I had just entered into university, but I had not yet reached eighteen at the time. I was excited about having entered into the school of my choice. I guess I was so excited to be out of my parents' hold that I threw caution into the wind. I decided to have a friend with benefits. We got tangled up so deep that at some point, we started having raw sex—when we were high on drugs. And then the next morning I would always take pills. I don't really remember how it happened that I forgot to take the one pill that would keep my life afloat. The next few weeks I felt something changing in me. I grew rounder and chubbier; I could get tired so fast. I knew something was up, so I went to see a doctor. I was pregnant. Those were the words I never thought I would ever say when I was that young. I was scared and confused; I didn't know who I could turn to. My whole world came crashing down on me so hard. I could barely breathe. When I told the guy responsible, he said I needed to get it out. I felt attached to my baby, so much. I could already imagine how it would have my eyes and nose and ears. She/he would have been beautiful, and I had to get rid of my baby. The thought weighed so heavily on me. I texted my mum and told her what was happening. She texted back the number of an abortionist. I was never so hurt as during that time. When I needed someone, I was all alone. I was depressed and drank a whole bottle of liquor to ease my pain, but all I felt was pain and darkness. The following day the guy responsible brought some pills that I had to take to abort my baby, but the drugs didn't work as required. I bled just a little, but the cramps were intense. After I went home for Christmas, I decided to go back to the hospital to get checked because I was having some weird discharge. They told me that my baby had died in my womb, and if I didn't get help soon I would get some complications. The doctor gave me pills to take and some to insert in my private part. I went home right after that. The pain I experienced for the next week was unbearable. I would prefer getting kicked and shot in the head to that. I was in anguish, knowing that I killed my baby. The physical pain was nothing compared to the emotional and mental pain. It never got easier; it never will. I have problems getting involved with people. I have problems getting attached to anyone. Most of the nights, I am sleepless, but I hope that I will one day get redemption and be happy again because right now it's the same as not living. I am a zombie who forces herself to wake up most mornings. People say it gets better. When?" Unnh! Obedience is better than the sacrifice–that may consume one's peace and leave one as pieces for life.

Distraction two – Early motherhood
Another distraction to students is early motherhood (to boys – early fatherhood). It is unplanned bridge in between academic and future dream. Sexual immorality among the unprepared students leads to teenage pregnancy. The distraction is much felt by the female students who could not abort the pregnancy. The mind will never enjoy peace because of the pain, shame, regret, loss, stigma, loneliness, loss of dream, and poverty that will

reduce the victim to nothing. It's never a happy time. The health matters in early motherhood and the state of mind of the victim can trigger up heart attack, high blood pressure, miscarriage, bleeding, etc.

Academically, early motherhood will affect the mother from concentrating in the class if she has the opportunity to school with the pregnancy. The rigorous work in the school will be too much for her. The shame may not allow easy assimilation. Therefore, shun what will distort your dream. Wait till you are ready to nurse a child with the best care as a successful person in your career. I will like to share with you another story of a teen mom who never knew she would be mother so early.[cxxxvi]

"I am currently 16 years old, reaching 17 in about a month. After noticing that I had missed my period, I originally thought nothing of it but soon I got morning sickness. That was when I knew that something was amiss. My tears nearly coursed their way down my cheeks as I asked my friend for help as I was underage, could you imagine an underage girl buying pregnancy kits? It had been confirmed that I was pregnant. I immediately sought help from my then boyfriend whom was utterly shocked by it as well. We had been having unprotected sex because he said that he was too lazy to get condoms (furthermore, he was underage as well) and that I would not get pregnant if he pulled out in time which he did every time. None of us had expected that result. Both of us sat in silence as we brood over the matter. He was keen on having an abortion while I was against it, it was a matter of life and death that we were talking about here but I was too afraid to face my parents and friends. Abortion was the only choice available to me. When we first had sex, he had told me that even if I got pregnant, he would settle down with me and raise the kid up with me even if he had to quit school and work to pay for the child's expenses. It was nothing more than a lie.

When he had finally convinced me of getting an abortion before my belly started to show, I heard some rumour about him. Apparently one of his 'brothers' (his close friend) had quarreled with him over me because apparently he had said something bad about me and his friend felt bad for me and tried to stand up for me. That was when I started to get suspicious of him as I knew that his friend was not one that would lie. He was an honest and down-to-earth guy and I trusted him. I lied to my boyfriend saying that I had gone for the abortion when I actually hadn't. Then one afternoon when he was bathing, I checked his phone. He actually had another girl behind my back as my entire world collapsed in that instant and inside their messages were things about me. Saying that "Don't worry babe, that dumb ***** went for an abortion already." I felt so cheated and angry, saddened at the same time as I immediately barged at him and slapped him. I stomped out of his house at once as he tried to pull me back but I got away from him as I rushed back home and cooped myself in my room , crying. My older brother, probably perturbed by my sobs, immediately confronted him as he nearly got a police case for assault.

I couldn't believe that I was being cheated by the man that I loved and cherished so much. Even more so when he called me a ***** behind my back. Just what did I mean to him? Was I just a ***** toilet to him through our entire relationship? Was I the only one that thought our love was real? That was when I spilled the beans of me being pregnant and that my brother was just standing up for me after seeing his beloved sister in tears. Ever since then, I haven't talked to him as news of me having a huge belly soon got to his ears. He tried to get me to forgive him as he had 'realized' his past mistakes but I was not going to fall for his two-faced ploy ever again. Right now, I am still not sure whether giving birth to his child was the right thing to do but seeing my baby's smile everyday itself was enough satisfying for me as I am taking turns with my family to take care of him as I return back to school after skipping school for an entire year."

Distraction three – Fashion trend
Fashion is a disease of generations. As countries of the world experience evolution, so also fashion does. It has outlived many generations and so it shall be. You cannot exhaust fashion. There

was a time we sewed 'old school' dress which came and gone for another style to come. All that we sew now has been before now. It is purely evolutional. Students in the school become the major victim of this trend. The latest fashion storms the campus. Some unwise will use their tuition, pocket money or borrowed money to get it at all cost, just to look nice in the school. If the way students run after fashion is the same way they run after reading, Africa would have become the best continent in the world. We are just stack consumers. Other continents formulate ideas, design style for fashion, and we purse and buy.

The trend of fashion has moved from covering the body to nudity. Every precious thing is hidden. Fashion that exposes your body is telling you that you are cheap and available for anyone. I stormed on an article posted on Facebook by Kibui Francis wall titled, *Precious Things Are Hidden.* [cxxxvii] I like to share with you. He wrote, "Two young ladies arrived at church wearing clothes that were revealing their body parts. Here is what the pastor told them: He took a good look at them and made them sit. Then he said something that, they might never forget in their life. He looked at them straight in the eyes and said, "Ladies, everything that God made valuable in this world is well covered and hard to see, find or get. Where do you find diamonds? Deep down in the ground, covered and protected. Where do you find pearls? Deep down at the bottom of the ocean, covered up and protected in a beautiful shell. Where do you find gold? Way down in the mine, covered over with layers of rock and to get them, you have to work hard and dig deep down to get them. He looked at them with serious eyes and said, "Your body is sacred and unique". "You are far more precious than gold, diamonds and pearls, and you should be covered too." So he added that, if you keep your treasured mineral just like gold, diamond and pearls, deeply covered up, a reputable mining organization with the requisite machinery will fly down and conduct years of extensive exploration. First, they will contact your government (family), sign professional contracts (wedding) and mine you professionally (legal marriage). But if you leave your precious minerals uncovered on the surface of the earth, you always attract a lot of illegal miners to come and mine you illegally. Everybody will just pick up their crude instruments and think they can dig you. Keep your bodies deeply covered so that they invite professional miners to chase you. Do you not know that your body is a temple of the Holy Spirit, who is in you, whom you have received from God? You are not your own; you were bought with a price."[cxxxviii] Bad dresses had made many ladies rape victims while some were kidnapped to Unknown Island either for forceful marriage or diabolical rituals. The way you dress is the way you will address. Some say "What you wear does not matter, it is your heart". They are wrong. The heart (mind) is the first decision factor of what you wear. Bad tree cannot bring forth good fruit. It shows you are bad.

Ahmad Muhammad Auwal, a columnist on an online Daily Trust Newspaper also expresses his opinion on immorality[cxxxix] that like other social vices such as drug abuse, cultism and prostitution, indecent dressing has become a major moral misconduct among students of Nigerian tertiary institutions. Indecent or crazy dressing, also known as "dress to kill" is rampant among universities, polytechnics and colleges of education students, particularly the females; all in the name of wanting to look "sexy," "sensuous," "tantalizing" and "stimulating," forgetting that they ought to look responsible instead. Wearing skimpy clothes, also known as "fitted," strapless and short blouses and sagging of trousers - "low waist" or "ass down," by boys and even girls, cleavages and sleeveless shirts, also known as "spaghetti or off-shoulder," are major moral problems associated with decency in dressing faced in tertiary institutions today.

Another university blogger[cxl] also describes the identity of boys in the campus that their pattern of dressing is different. It makes them to look so dirty and also unattractive with unkempt hairs and dirty jeans having pockets of holes deliberately created around the knees and the lower parts of the trousers allowed to flow on the ground because they go through their heels into their legs as socks. The waist of their trousers are lowered and fastened tightly at the middle of the two bottom lobes to reveal their boxers (pants). And when they are walking, they drag their legs and one of their hands particularly the left one, cupping their invisible scrotum as if they will fall to the ground if not supported. As godly and future-minded student, you have choice to live above all these abnormalities. Your mind has all that you need to be the best. Allow it. Do not distract your mind for useless impression of fashion called craziness of the age.

Distraction four – Music madness

Music is healing for soul. Many lives have been encouraged, inspired and got moving as a result of good music. Music and learning go together sometimes. Students love music. Yet music without control is not needed. As student, you need to answer these questions about the music you listen to: What is the music all about? Does it inspire you to be a better person in your lifestyle? Who sang the song? Do you have good understanding of the lyrics? Are you crazy about the music or less moved? Do you love to imitate the lifestyle of the singer? Is there any positive impact of the singer on the society? Can you wish the private life of the singer yours?

The musicians that do not portray modesty and godliness are not worth following. Some have become celebrities for students. Aminah Oyeleye and Seliat Lawalon on The Nation Online Newspaper[cxli] add their view that indecent dressing is common among celebrities, particularly among artistes. This set of people, while on stage will want to look unique and in the process turned themselves into lunatic and you dressed like them. Some lyrics are not educating. Beware of music that rhythms overshadow the lyrics. Do not be addicted to songs that do not inspire you for readings, studying, inventing new things. Do not cram songs to the detriments of your reading. You primary assignment is your book, not lyrics books. Songs can dictate your actions if you do not define your choice. As from now, be simple and godly over songs. Do not enjoy what you are not supposed to listen to. Give you mind to music that encourages modesty, resonance, peace, usefulness and invention.

Distraction five – Pride

What do you have that you are not given? Is it your body, shape, clothe, intelligence, riches, power, fame, etc.? You are a product of somebody's commitment. God gave man opportunity to be what he is today. Pride makes a student to look down on anyone as if they are nobody. It is the matter of your mind. Pride distracts your attention from necessary things to irrelevance. The time you use to adore your beauty behind mirror can be used to prepare yourself for examination. I discovered most adorned female students never win any prestigious prizes or awards in the school.[cxlii] I may be wrong. If not, prove me right with your action. The gold-mind dedicates time to learn from others, but the proud one never gives attention to anything than his ambitious mission to the top. Pride of what you know can kill what you had known. You will not go beyond what you had known if pride is your logo.

Do you teach others what you know? Do you bend to learn more? Do you admire or appreciate another person's work? Do you envy anyone's progress? If you do, you are not helping your studentship. Ignore what you are, to be what you dream to be. Celebrate other better than yourself so that you can be celebrated also. Strive to share knowledge, academic material, money, kindness and love with other students.

Distraction six – Technological misuse

Nigeria and other African countries love technology because it makes life easier and better every day. Every student has access to technology in different forms and it helps to solve daily problems in the school world. Technology has more advantage when it is connected to internet. There are millions of people on the internet who are searching to meet other people in order to gather information and share experiences on a variety of topics. Because of this, hundreds of social networking sites and apps have been created, and they have attracted millions of users in the few short years that social networking has become a phenomenon. The sites and apps also vary the ways in which they show and incorporate new information and communication tools, like mobile access, blogging, and photo and video sharing.[cxliii]

However, technology that makes studentship easier can also distract. When it becomes addiction, the necessary usage is lost. Social networking addiction is a behavioural addiction. Because social networking interaction can lead to elevation in moods, one may make the connection that social networking addiction is a disease. According to Rose, an online analyst on social media addiction,[cxliv] She notes that, "The following are some of the most categorized symptoms of social networking addiction:

- Your social networking activities cause you to neglect your obligations such as reading, studying, housework and school work.
- You lose track of time when you're on sites like Twitter, Facebook, or apps like Whatsapp.
- Your social networking activities have caused negative issues at work or school, yet you continue those activities.
- You sleep less, and avoid sleep regardless of fatigue, to spend time on sites like Facebook.
- You create an enhanced online personality-unrelated to your real person.
- You increasingly share information or become a part of online activities and discussions you know are dangerous like pages for malpractices–live exam papers and answers–porn page, romantic sites, etc.
- You lie about relationships to encourage more interaction online by other users.
- You spend more time socializing online, and begin to avoid person to person interactions.
- You are too preoccupied with the posts of those you follow.
- You begin to lie as you chat in order to add excitement to your Facebook and Twitter wall."

I know of a girl whose phone fell off and was damaged. She burst into cry – deep cry. Why? She would not be able to ping her friends again."[cxlv] She did not cry for inability to browse for solution and sites for assignments and projects. This is evil and addiction. Our mind needs guard. Watch out for anything that fills your minds on social media sites. Do not be desperate about friendship online. Only be curious to know more about people, knowledge and sites that will link you up with your future.

Distraction seven – Cultism

Cultism can be defined as a ritual practice by a group of people whose membership, admission, policy and initiation formalities as well as their mode of operations are done in secret and kept secret with their activities having negative effects on both members and non-members alike.[cxlvi] It was introduced into academic institutions more than five decades ago. Through Wikipedia and Adewale Rotimi in his paper, *Violence in the Citadel: The Menace of Secret Cults in the Nigerian Universities*[cxlvii] expounded the origin of this evil in our school in Nigeria. In 1952, future-Nobel Prize winning author Wole Soyinka and a group of six friends formed the Pyrate Confraternity at the elite University College, Ibadan, and then part of the University of London. According to the Pyrates, the "Magnificent Seven", as they called themselves, observed that the university was populated with wealthy students associated with the colonial powers and a few poorer students striving in manner and dress to be accepted by the more advantaged students, while social life was dictated by tribal affiliation. Soyinka would later note that the Pyrates wanted to differentiate themselves from "stodgy establishment and its pretentious products in a new educational institution different from a culture of hypocritical and affluent middleclass, different from alienated colonial aristocrats". The organization adopted the motto *"Against all conventions"*, the skull and crossbones as their logo, while members adopted confraternity names such as "Cap'n Blood" and "Long John Silver". Membership was open to any promising male student, regardless of tribe or race, but selection was stringent and most applicants were denied. For almost 20 years, the Pyrates were the only confraternity on Nigerian campuses.

After this group had received popularity, others groups erupted from other schools. The Supreme Eiye Confraternity (also known as the National Association of Air Lords) was formed in the University of Ibadan in 1965. In the 1980s confraternities spread throughout the over 300 institutions of higher education in the country. The Neo-Black Movement of Africa (also called Black Axe) emerged from the University of Benin in Edo State. In 1983 students at the University of Calabar in Cross River State founded the Eternal Fraternal Order of the Legion Consortium (the Klan Konfraternity, the Supreme Vikings Confraternity (the Adventurers or, alternately, the De Norsemen Club of Nigeria) the following year. This time period saw a drastic change in the role of the confraternities. The coup of Ibrahim Babangida in 1983 caused a large degree of political tension. Military leaders, beginning in the 1980s, began to see the confraternities as a check on the student unions and university staff, who were the only organized groups opposing military rule. The confraternities were thus provided payment and weapons to use against student activists, though the weapons were often used in deadly inter-confraternity rivalries. Sociologist Emeka Akudi[cxlviii] noted that some university vice-chancellors protected confraternities which were known to be violent and used them to attack students deemed troublesome. During this period the confraternities introduced a new tradition of carrying out traditional religious practices, including Vodun, before any other activity.

The old long evil has become a great threat on education in Africa. The cult members are witch-hunted by security agencies because of their evil atrocities committed day by day in schools and society. Any cult member has no gut/freedom to make his identity known - it is always uncommunicative. Adewale Rotimi asserts that secret cult is not a new phenomenon in Africa, but what is new is the recent violence consistently associated with it. Today, the operations of cult groups in our tertiary institutions is accompanied with violence, maiming, killing and different types of anti-social activities.[cxlix]

The consequences of cultism on individuals are as follows: You will live in perpetual bondage and fear. This is because cultists are always watching their backs because rival cults are always at 'war'. Cultists are always destructive, merciless, stubborn and wicked; so a well-mannered individual that indulges in cultism will automatically transform his good behavior to an ill-behaved person. Most cultists have no regards for moral and values. As a result of one belonging to a cult, he/she will lose respect for that which is morally right, e.g. respect for elders. Premature death may occur because cultist is liable to die young. There is possible expulsion from school.[cl] The mind of the victim will also lose its peace. Cultism is a distraction to learning. I plead with you to shun and preach against it. Your future is more important than power and fame you will get from confraternity. They are temporal. If the pioneers do not have pleasure in this group again; then be disciplined. Face your studies with all seriousness. Your seat on the top is still available. Be proactive and pragmatic in your reading and studying.

CHAPTER NINE

MANAGEMENT OF DEPRESSION IN THE MIND OF STUDENT

Depression is in every place where there are breath-taking events such as poverty, economic meltdown, suicide bombing, kidnapping, long time illness, failure, natural disaster, disappointment, unemployment and others. Most men live to manage this menace as they can with self-medication, self-philosophy, hopeless expectation and psyche-traditional drugs and myths. So also in the students' world is this menace. According to World Health Organization (WHO)[cli] explains that depression is a common mental disorder that presents with depressed mood, loss of interest or pleasure, feelings of guilt or low self-worth, disturbed sleep or appetite, low energy, and poor concentration. The stress of studying within and outside the school also has great effect on students' mind. What to eat, drink, wear, spend or use has influence on the state of mind of students. The school system, the lecturers' palaver, teachers' method of teaching, load of assignment, social life, financial support, health and others can cause a student to feel depressed and lose mind. It is purely psychological.

According to Dallard and Miller[clii] (paraphrased by me), if a student lives with criticism, he learns to condemn. If a student lives with insecurity, he learns to lose faith in himself. If a student lives with rejection, he learns to hate. If a student lives with fear, he learns to be apprehensive. If a student lives with blame, he learns to ignore a goal. If a student lives with pity, he learns to be sorry for himself. If a student lives with disapproval, he learns to dislike himself. If a student lives with jealousy, he learns to feel guilty. All these can stress out learning from you if not managed. Student has stress when load of works is too much. The physical bodies of students can handle normal stress, but when it becomes excessive the health suffers.

When depression catches up with a student, the learning becomes difficult. The student begins to exhibit signs and symptoms such as: loss of interest in activities that were once interesting or enjoyable–reading and studying–; loss of appetite with weight loss or overeating with weight gain; loss of emotional expression; a persistently sad, anxious or empty mood; feelings of hopelessness, pessimism, guilt, worthlessness, or helplessness; social withdrawal; unusual fatigue, low energy level, a feeling of being slowed down; sleep disturbance with sleeplessness, early-morning awakening, or oversleeping; trouble concentrating, remembering, or making decisions; unusual restlessness or irritability; persistent physical problems such as headaches, digestive disorders, or chronic pain that do not respond to treatment; thoughts of death or suicide attempts.[cliii] However, all these symptoms have roots and they shall be dealt with in this chapter one after the other.

Depression one – Failure

Failure is not a disease; it is a pause for checkup. Failure is a test on your capacity, endurance and tolerance. "When I fail, I try again,"–This is the tone of successful people who was once a student. Failure weakens mind and leads to depression that will totally sap health to zero. Depression soars on the wing of student who has believed that he cannot make it again. Let's read through the profile of great men and women who were once failure but today everyone celebrates their invention, discoveries and endurance because they did not give up. All these stories that were highlighted below[cliv] [clv] are to encourage you that great men also failed, but they refused to remain failure.

Abraham Lincoln:

As a young man, Abraham Lincoln went to war a captain and returned a private. Afterwards, he was a failure as a businessman. As a lawyer in Springfield, he was too impractical and temperamental to be a success. He turned to politics and was defeated in his first try for the legislature, again defeated in his first attempt to be nominated for congress, defeated in his application to be commissioner of the General Land Office, defeated in the senatorial election of 1854, defeated in his efforts for the vice-presidency in 1856, and defeated in the senatorial election of 1858. At about that time, he wrote in a letter to a friend, "I am now the most miserable man living. If what I feel were equally distributed to the whole human family, there would not be one cheerful face on the earth." While today he is remembered as one of the greatest leaders of world and president of US.

Sigmund Freud:

He was hissed from the podium when he first presented his ideas to the scientific community of Europe. He returned to his office and kept on writing. Later he became the father of psychotherapy and psychology.

Thomas Edison:

Thomas Edison's teachers said he was "too stupid to learn anything." He was fired from his first two jobs for being "non-productive." As an inventor, Edison made 1,000 unsuccessful attempts at inventing the light bulb. When a reporter asked, "How did it feel to fail 1,000 times?" Edison replied, "I didn't fail 1,000 times. The light bulb was an invention with 1,000 steps."

Bill Gates:

Gates didn't seem like a shoe-in for success after dropping out of Harvard and starting a failed first business with Microsoft co-founder Paul Allen called Traf-O-Data. While this early idea didn't work, Gates' later did work, creating the global empire that is Microsoft.

Harland David Sanders:

Perhaps better known as Colonel Sanders of Kentucky Fried Chicken fame. Sanders had a hard time selling his chicken at first. In fact, his famous secret chicken recipe was rejected 1,009 times before a restaurant accepted it.

Walt Disney:

Today Disney rakes in billions from merchandise, movies and theme parks around the world, but Walt Disney himself had a bit of a rough start. He was fired by a newspaper editor because, "he lacked imagination and had no good ideas." After that, Disney started a number of businesses that didn't last too long and ended with bankruptcy and failure. He kept plugging along, however, and eventually found a recipe for success that worked.

Albert Einstein:

Most of us take Einstein's name as synonymous with genius, but he didn't always show such promise. Einstein did not speak until he was four and did not read until he was seven, causing his teachers and parents to think he was mentally handicapped, slow and anti-social. Eventually, he was expelled from school and was refused admittance to the Zurich Polytechnic School. It might have taken him a bit longer, but most people would agree that he caught on pretty well in the end, winning the Nobel Prize and changing the face of modern physics.

Charles Darwin:

In his early years, Darwin gave up on having a medical career and was often chastised by his father for being lazy and too dreamy. Darwin himself wrote, "I was considered by all my masters and my father, a very ordinary boy, rather below the common standard of intellect." Perhaps they judged too soon, as Darwin today is well-known for his scientific studies - theory of evolution.

Robert Goddard:

Goddard today is hailed for his research and experimentation with liquid-fueled rockets, but during his lifetime his ideas were often rejected and mocked by his scientific peers who thought they were outrageous and impossible. Today rockets and space travel don't seem far-fetched at all, due largely in part to the work of this scientist who worked against the feelings of the time.

Isaac Newton:

Newton was undoubtedly a genius when it came to math, but he had some failings early on. He never did particularly well in school and when put in charge of running the family farm, he failed miserably, so poorly in fact that an uncle took charge and sent him off to Cambridge where he finally blossomed into the scholar we know today.

Orville and Wilbur Wright:

These brothers fought depression and family illness before starting the bicycle shop that would lead them to experimenting with flight. After numerous attempts at creating flying machines, several years of hard work, and tons of failed prototypes, the brothers finally created a plane that could get airborne and stay there.

Winston Churchill:

This Nobel Prize-winning, twice-elected Prime Minster of the United Kingdom wasn't always as well regarded as he is today. Churchill struggled in school and failed the sixth grade. After school he faced many years of political failures, as he was defeated in every election for public office until he finally became the Prime Minister at the ripe old age of 62.

J. K. Rowling:

Rowling may be rolling in a lot of Harry Potter dough today, but before she published the series of novels she was nearly penniless, severely depressed, divorced, trying to raise a child on her own while attending school and writing a novel. Rowling went from depending on welfare to survive to being one of the richest women in the world in a span of only five years through her hard work and determination.

Ludwig van Beethoven:

In his formative years, young Beethoven was incredibly awkward on the violin and was often so busy working on his own compositions that he neglected to practice. Despite his love of composing, his teachers felt he was hopeless at it and would never succeed with the violin or in composing. Beethoven kept plugging along, however, and composed some of the best-loved symphonies of all time–five of them while he was completely deaf.

Michael Jordan:

Most people wouldn't believe that a man often lauded as the best basketball player of all time was actually cut from his high school basketball team. Luckily, Jordan didn't let this setback stop him from playing the game that he has stated, "I have missed more than 9,000 shots in my career. I have lost almost 300 games. On 26 occasions I have been entrusted to take the game winning shot, and I missed. I have failed over and over and over again in my life. And that is why I succeed."

I also curled out these quotes from these great minds that failed but refused to remain as failure.[clvi]

- "Ever tried. Ever failed. No matter. Try Again. Fail again. Fail better." - Samuel Beckett
- "Our greatest glory is not in never-falling but in rising every time we fall." - Confucius
- Great success is built on failure, frustration, even catastrophe." - Sumner Redstone
- "Failing is one of the greatest arts in the world. One fails toward success." - Charles Kettering
- "Failure provides the opportunity to begin again, more intelligently." - Henry Ford
- "The fastest way to succeed is to double your failure rate." - Thomas Watson Sr.
- "Only those who dare to fail greatly can achieve greatly." - Robert F. Kennedy
- "Our achievements speak for themselves. What we have to keep track of are our failures, discouragements, and doubts. We tend to forget the past difficulties, the many false starts, and the painful groping. We see our past achievements as the end result of a clean forward thrust, and our present difficulties as signs of decline and decay." - Eric Hoffer
- "The essential part of creativity is not being afraid to fail." - Edwin Land
- "I don't believe I have special talents, I have persistence ... After the first failure, second failure, third failure, I kept trying." - Carlo Rubbia, Nobel Prize winning Physicist

- "No matter how hard you work for success, if your thought is saturated with the fear of failure, it will kill your efforts, neutralize your endeavors and make success impossible." - Baudjuin
- "Little minds are tamed and subdued by misfortune; but great minds rise above them." - Washington Irving
- "Every great cause is born from repeated failures and from imperfect achievements." - Maria Montessori

How to conquer depression of failure as students

The mind of student is the first seat of success and failure. If you believe you can make it, then work hard and ignore failure. Master your failure as numerous steps that will not work out. Let your reading be focused on what you need first. Decide to live above stress that will reduce you assimilating power. Be yourself. Talk with someone about your failure and seek advice to improve your shortcomings. Do not pretend to be successful when you are not. Discuss what you do not know with whoever that knows it. Review and revise your tests, assignment, exams, and projects before the next exams. Be frank with your excesses that do not add to you. Finally, Pray to God as you read and prepare for examination and your dreams.

Depression two – Fear

Fear is the picture that mind produces when there is sense of insecurity and threat. Fear is the opposite of faith and confidence. Fear of tomorrow, fear of uncertainty, fear of examinations, fear of evil, etc. are dangerous for the mind of students. Fear can make a strong, brilliant and social student to stay in-door for days because of the pictures he perceives which no one else sees. Whenever you allow fear to stay, your physical strength will collapse - the ability in yourself will also fall. The hands that write well may also lose strength because of fear.

Why do students live in fear?

- Student that presumes and imagines evil in heart will suffer fear.

- Student who did evil in the past or on revenge mission will live in fear of nemesis.
- Whenever the pang hands of conscience grips a student, the consciousness of fear will fill the air.
- Unpreparedness of students for exam and test breeds fear.
- When a student had attempted wrong actions like unprotected sex, abortion, malpractices, murder, stealing or rape.
- Secret and private lifestyle can accommodate fear.
- Darkness around the school may cause fear. When a student has phobia for darkness, fear will show forth.
- Fear to attempt a project, classwork or presentation.
- Fear of audience.

This fear of audience leads me to search for more reasons and why students shy away from public presentation. Do you know that God made you perfect with internal strength to stand tall and bold at all times? Yes, He did, but you refuse to see what you are. There was a story of a boy[clvii] who was listed to lead an invocation in programme where fifty thousand people were on seat. He was afraid when he saw the crowd through a corner. He moved to the master of the programme to check again for the order and to his surprise he saw his name as the speaker of the programme. He lost his breath and could not believe his head. He protested that "I just can't do that, to make a speech to a big crowd unprepared, I'm not. Someone else will have to speak in my place". There was an elderly man called Colonel Roosevelt who watched the fearful boy. He said, "Are you afraid?" "Yes, more than that, to face a crowd unprepared?" the boy relied. Colonel Roosevelt responded, "For one thing, stop telling yourself that you are scared and start thinking courage. Practice affirming confidence. Another thing, I suggest that you stop thinking of yourself – your lack of eloquence, colour of your face". He took the boy to one side to see the crowd very well and shown him a group of mothers that their sons died during war. He asserted, "Forget yourself and anyone in the crowd and focus on the bereaved mothers. You can do it. Look, boy, all the resources you need are in your mind. You can draw them out with confidence. Relax, start thinking and it will come to you."" Immediately, fear and uncertainty disappeared and he gained confidence to speak expressly. You also can. Speak with a friend or counselor about your situation. It is part of learning. You learn best when you daily discover what you could not do and giving it the best approach to get it well.

Fear is believing a lie, listening to negative voices, and not taking God at His word. What did God tell you about your future? Do you believe God that He can never lie? If yes, deal with fear of future with prayer and confession of faith.[clviii] Fear strangles divinity in you. I mean the word of God you know in you. My son one day wanted to ease himself in the toilet, though everywhere was dark. He went a few distances and returned. Why did you return? I asked him. "Fear!" he replied. I told him, "God is with you". He said, "Yes I know He is with me but not in the toilet."[clix] I laughed and still got surprised that fear can make a a child denies the potency of God. Fear can disable a man and an army. Fear can dismantle a country. In the Bible, when four lepers left their home to search for food, the host of soldiers of Syria fled the battle field because they heard the sound of great warriors like rumour of war.[clx] That is what fear can do.

I had experience of fear in 2014 when I was to leave the city of Minna, Nigeria to another city that was yet defined and unknown to me. My mind started thinking of many possibilities and impossibilities and nearly strangled the move. I took a bold step to move on when my plans failed still. Today, I thanked God that I tramped fear on my feet.[clxi] Praise God.

How to quit depression of fear as students

Fear is not real, confront it. It is false evidence appearing real; arise on your feet to disperse it. When you are afraid, do the thing you are afraid of and soon you will lose fear of it. Take a long, straight look at your fear. Know what causes the fear; for self-knowledge and insight into the matter will overcome fear. Are they your tests and examinations that depressed you? Great heroes also did exam. Your parents also passed theirs. Believe in God and your preparation. Forget about the past that threatens your effort. Believe that you are passing well this time around. Talk out your fear with loud voice, it will run. Talk also with a Christian friend about your fear. As a Christian, I believe in the name of Jesus because darkness of fear cannot stay in His presence. You can try it also, for it works.

Depression three – Grief

Sadness or grief from the death or loss of a loved one, though natural, can also increase the risk of depression in students. Grief is heart-touching situation, an emotional response to death of a loved one. Vladimir Putin, Russian President and politician, in August 22, 2000, while meeting with families of the Russian sailors who died in the Kursk submarine disaster made this statement and I quote that, "The grief is immeasurable; there are not enough words of comfort. My heart hurts, but yours hurt even more".[clxii] There is no word or sympathy that can console such person except God. How does it affect students? Whenever a student loses his/her parent, siblings, close friends, spouse, financiers, mentor or colleagues, there is a deep depression on the mind. Many messages will fill the mind such as: "No more hope", "It is over", "No one can understand me again", "Who will be there for me again?", "I will quit the race", etc. Sincerely, grief creates holes in the heart of the student and may nearly disrupt learning system if not managed.

The grief of financiers or sponsors which may be the parents or guardians usually affects the mind against learning. In this situation, you are to look unto God for consolation. Be grateful to God for His plan for you. Giving up at the time is not the best option. The deed is done. Two losses do not make you a better person. You need to understand what has happened. In your moment of calmness and deep thought, be pragmatic on the matter and prayerfully table another plan B on board. You need a reliable and consoling relative/friend at this time. If you have a friend in this situation, invite other students or elderly to talk with the bereaved. Allow the person to express himself. The goal is not to take away the pain of grief, but to allow an opportunity for the person to express the pain. Avoid comments aimed at trying to cheer up the grieving students. Your presence makes a great relief for the person. Reach out to the family for more help. After the moment of grief, provide learning supports for the fellow student. A friend in deed is a friend in need.

Depression four – Assimilation problem

Most students have this challenge of retaining what is read over a period. Assimilating[clxiii] is a learning process that integrates new knowledge or information with what is already known into the brain for use. I have seen students reading just to pass examination. Some even memorize the textbook to pour down as the teacher taught in the class. That is why Nigeria is raising incompetent graduates that cannot defend their certificates. This problem can become depressive for students if it is managed. It is expected of a student to grab whatever is taught in the class but the strength of each student differs. We have slow and fast leaners. However, this problem goes with the slow learner.

What to do:

According to Bill Klemm, these are helpful guide to better assimilation during reading. [clxiv] It is advised to read with a purpose. Eliminate distractions. Speed-read first. Get the reading mechanics right. Be judicious in highlighting and note taking. Mark up the text. Think in pictures. Rehearse as you go along. Stay within your attention span and work to increase that span. Write a few sentences of summary at the bottom of each page. Write down questions that you have about what you read. Create impression for your reading. For example, you can stop reading one second and picture the situation in your mind, exaggerating some features of the situation in order to enhance the impression of your mental image, by adding passion, greatness, or anything to shock yourself. You can even add yourself in your mental picture, imagining President Mohammadu Buhari[clxv] thanking you for your help or anything memorable. This will make the impression stronger. Rehearse again soon. If you do this concurrently your assimilation will move on until you master your reading. You can also study chapter six of this book again.

Depression five – Hatred

Depression of hatred is too much to bear for students. It comes from different angles, either from self or others. Having a strong dislike for oneself is like rejecting the sixth day work of God. Self-hatred may come up when you fail your target or commit a crime against your will. Hatred is evil. Your mind will suffer most because you will not appreciate the best of life except sad ones. Failure of exam or target in life must not lower your personality, dream and aspiration. I have this word for you from the renowned Neurosurgeon; Dr. Ben Carson. He wrote this beautiful piece,[clxvi] "Sometimes you are unsatisfied with your life, while many people in this world are dreaming of living your life. A child on a farm sees a plane fly overhead and dreams of flying. But, a pilot on the plane sees the farmhouse and dreams of returning home. That's life!! Enjoy yours. If wealth is the secret to happiness, then the rich should be dancing on the streets. But only poor kids do that. If power ensures security, then officials should walk unguarded. But those who live simply sleep soundly. If beauty and fame bring ideal relationships, then celebrities should have the best marriages. But those who live simply walk humbly and love genuinely! All good will come back to you!!! Man asks, "Where was God when Myles Munroe,[clxvii] wife and his associates were killed in a crash? He answers, "The same place I sat when John the Baptist my servant was beheaded. When Stephen my servant was stoned to death. When Paul my servant was murdered in Rome. The same place I sat when my only Son was brutally crucified, wounded, bruised and killed. I have not moved from my position." I am the same. It is not the means of exit from earth that matters but the destination. Live simply. It's all about God!!" Love God. Love yourself.

Hatred generated from other people like friends, lecturers, parents or siblings can also cause depression. What can stir up this kind of hatred? It may be that your output is lowered to your parent's expectation or your character is causing damage to their reputation. Indecent lifestyle can make friends to dislike one. In another way, envying of one's progress can cause hatred. Resentment and hate will also have their demonstrated place in the bad health picture.[clxviii] A long-term hate has tendency to cause damage to critical organs of the body.

What to do:

Discover the reason for the hatred. Be dissatisfied with the status quo. If it is self-hatred, forgive yourself. Love yourself. Try to re-appreciate your good side and work on your weakness that makes you sober and sad. Talk to someone that can help you – a counsellor or minister of God. Be optimistic and proactive about the issue. Do not postpone the talk. It may affect your learning activities in the school. If you hate someone, forgive the persons also. You can talk to someone that will link both of you for reconciliatory talk. If the matter is your fault, take to correction and improve your life to meet up the expectations. No one is 100% wrong and 100% right; there will be at least 5% better or worse side. Any unsolved issue of hatred will grow into mind cancer that may stop your intellectual dream and future career. Let me tell you this: Love is the opposite of hatred. You must replace hatred with love in your mind as you study in your school. Jesus was hated by His people, yet He prayed for them, "Father, forgive them, for they do not know what they do."[clxix]

Depression six – Regret and guilt from the past

Depression is not good for the mind. When you have the past in your memory, it has power to blind you from the future. Truly, there is no one without the past – past error, sin, disappointment, etc. We live in the world that mistake is not prohibited. Yet, we live on to forget the past. Students who had serial abortions may suffer guilt when she hears the cry of innocent babies. Also a cultist who had killed innocent souls will always feel uncomfortable when such issue comes alive even after he has changed his ways. Regret can lead a student to coma–academic coma–I mean a stand-still on learning activities. The mood will change. The social life will shell up. The health, the blood pressure and temperature will rise above normal. Why? Because you allow past to hold you down. Great heroes also had 'past mistakes' that are worse than yours. If we have conference of 'past lives', then we will know the grand commander victim of the 'past'. Charles F. Kettering, the great inventive genius, once remarked, "I am not interested in the past. I am only interested in the future, for that is where I expect to spend the rest of my life."[clxx] Guilt about the past is setback to mind's activities. Come to the saving grace in Jesus Christ now.

What to do:

God has given peace through sacrifice of Jesus Christ to cancel all the past.[clxxi] If you have opportunity to seek for God's forgiveness and you also forgive yourself, the depression will gradually die out of your life. Now, begin to imagine different and better picture of your life. Start developing what is called rightness in thinking. Reset priority with future-oriented plans. Though you cannot delete your past, yet you can see goodness from it. Your past should be a lesson for you when anyone is about to fall victim of the evil you did. Let joy and peace fill your mind whenever regret and guilt come. Have a plan for the future. Nothing in life is more exciting and rewarding than the sudden flash of insight that leaves you a changed person - not only changed, but changed for the better.[clxxii] If devil cannot keep you away from your past, he must not take away your joy and fulfillment. Therefore, see the world that needs your impact – your dream career. Do not weary your mind with forgotten past. When you talk the past let it be that you are preaching or counseling.

Depression seven – Rejection

Rejection is setback in the mind. It comes when you feel people around you do not want you alive, active or successful. This kind of thought is real. Many students have been rejected and abandoned by parents, friends and colleagues for no reasons. Sometimes, the reason is neither genuine nor tenable for the act of rejection. Rejection of one's personality is the worst of all depressions. Opposite of rejection is appreciation. When last did you appreciate yourself after examinations? Have you ever appreciated your little effort when you failed a course below your set target? Do you compare yourself with genius or average ones in the class? Do you trust the wealth of your mind when others talk in the class? If we develop greater appreciation of the immense resources built into the mind, we can do amazing things – even greater than we dare to imagine. What a student can be and what he can do is largely determined by the degree of self-limitation which he mentally imposes on himself. If he images himself on a restless level, the flow of resources from the mind will be reduced and maintained at a tickle of the full potential.[clxxiii]

Where you are does not hold you down to where you are going. What is in you is the main catalyst that will differentiate you from others. Do not look down on yourself. I have a story of an eagle that initially lost identity to rejection but gainfully had it after appreciation of its uniqueness. There was the story of an eaglet who thought it was a chicken.[clxxiv] One day, an adventurous young boy climbed high in the mountains and found an eagle's nest. He picked one egg and put it with the chicken eggs in the farm. The hen hacked the eggs and out came a little eaglet along with the chicks. The eaglet was raised with the chickens and it never knew it was anything else but a chicken. It lived a normal life like others. But as it began to grow there were strange stirrings within it. It rejected the urge as nothing. Every once in a while it would think, "There must be more to me than chicken!" But it never did anything about until one day tremendous eagle flew over the chicken yard. The eaglet felt strange new strength in its wings. It became aware of an enormous heartbeat, still felt unworthy to fly so far it had been on the ground for long. That is rejection at work. It said, "I cannot do that, even if I try, no one will believe me that I can". The eagle never gave up flying around the farm until the eaglet change its mind as it watched the eagle the thought came, "I'm like that. A chicken yard is not for me. I want to climb the sky and perch on mountains". Then it took off gradually, flew high and high till it disappears into the blue sky (paraphrased). Nobody can be truly you or act on your behalf or push you to action if you have not appreciated your worth from the mind to the body.

A student with rejection will also reject God's offer of love. There will be doubt of acceptance and forgiveness when such student sins against God. To plead for mercy will be difficult. Jesus has never rejected anyone no matter the sins, error, or mistakes. His hand is wide open to give rest. There was a family with a child that was confirmed as a slow child. He would probably never learn to read much and would end up with emotional problem. If you were this child what will you do? Would you not have committed suicide? The parent did not reject the boy. One day the mother said to the boy, "You have a problem. Now I know you can overcome this problem but more important, you must believe you can overcome it." The boy replied, "Mama, I'm afraid to try, I've failed so much trying to learn to read I'm afraid to fail. I'm rejected by all". The mother concluded, "Things are different now, you have me help and you and I together have Jesus. He will never reject you if you never reject yourself too."[clxxv] Do you have a rejected friend? How do you add to the rejection? Your faith in the student's ability will boost his confidence to also believe in God.

Some people think that rejection is worse when it comes from someone you know, trust and love, but sometimes it can hurt deeply when it is from people you are meeting for the first time.[clxxvi] It becomes worst when you experience rejection from your biological parents. In 1995, my friend who was deeply depressed at school had rejection from home. The father used to beat him with anything and anytime, whenever he arrived home around one o clock in the midnight from beer parlour. This boy could not believe his head that his biological father could treat him so bad. One day, the father naked him and about to knock him down with hammer, then my friend jumped out of the house in the dark night in which only God saved him from the hand of ritualists that night. The step mother also did not help the situation. She cared for her daughter at the expense of my friend and his sister. Sometimes, he would eat 'Garri' and *'kulikuli'* as breakfast. He would trek to school with taunted school uniform and loose mind of what to eat during break time. This situation caused him to shun class for bad friends. He repeated twice and almost lost his dream of future. This is rejection from parents. Today, God has vindicated him and placed him in his dream–now he is a Chattered Insurer in a big company with his family–because he did not give up. I too was available for him as an encourager and prayer partner. You too can do the same for somebody. Accept yourself. Believe yourself. Count on yourself. Deny wrong premonition about rejection. Encourage the victim of rejection. Friendship with him/her who rejected you is a healing for the both.

Depression eight – Ideas without support
"I have a dream, a song to sing..." was sung by a group of American singers many years ago. I know that some students may also sing the song this way, *"I have ideas but... no support."* This is a big pain in the bone of the mind. When a person burnt candle to unravel ideas that would save humanity from stress and give better life but the matter of supports grounded the script. This kind of mind will be regretful to attempt anything again. Most students that are intelligent, resourceful and inventive have lost morale to continue due to the depression of lack of supports. Though Government inaugurated many support schemes for entrepreneurial ideas but how many of the youth and students were given this opportunity? Only the well-connected ones have it all. God has better plan for His children. Giving up at this time will not save your passion. You need to personally encourage yourself. Don't you know that idea does not die? It may sleep for long; it shall wake up alive in a day. Always remember that ideas outlive the idealist.

Keep record of your write ups, designs, web works, sculptural work, articles, art works, painting, inventions, poems, storylines, policies, formula, principles, and others. An artistic student can keep his inventions for a future exhibition that may promote the good work. Keep the spirits glowing. Talk to yourself that support is on the way. If you are students that do well in the class and the parents do not appreciate you, do not give up. I know of a girl whose parent never appreciated her good results and whenever she brought it worst result, she would be beaten mercilessly. She later concluded to keep failing. She said, "When I do well, no praise; and when I fail, it is lashes, then I will fail more to provoke the beaten, I lose nothing."

You can encourage your mind to continually be industrious, creative, diligent and inventive no matter the shortage of support. You can search for relevant groups, team or NGO who support such work online. Visit seminars, workshop and training centers for connections. Do not hide you findings; it is only the work that is known publicly that will make you known. Organize talk, programmes, social exhibition to showcase your worth. You can raise donations for your work. When you try to help yourself, then supporters will come to assist, therefore do something. Stop being moody, pitiable, weak and dull. Revitalize your creativity now. Let your mind see greater tomorrow.

Depression nine – Spiritual problems

Continuous and consistent experience of sadness and failure on the learning activities of student that has no scientific proof is likely to be spiritual. We are in the world of power. Bible says, "We are not fighting against flesh and blood"[clxxvii], "and the weapon of our warfare is not carnal, but mighty in God…"[clxxviii] When you are depressed unknowingly, you need to seek the face of God for help. Student that reads without understanding consistently, even after all the psychological therapy for assimilation had been done, needs help and deliverance from his Maker, Jesus Christ. Spiritual problems may be bad luck, night mare, bad dreams, consistent hatred, evil thought and desire, seducing passion, unexplained rejection, suicidal thought, hopelessness, etc. All these signal to the wicked work of the enemy over your life. There is no psychological formula that can solve spiritual problems.

What to do:

First, you need God as your Lord. Second, you need to accept the victory of Christ over all powers, for it is written concerning Him that, "He is the head of all dominions or principalities or powers..."[clxxix], and "In His name all knees shall bow and every tongue shall confess Jesus is Lord..."[clxxx] Third, you need unwavering faith in your heart. Fourth, pray without ceasing. The kingdom of God suffers violence and the violent take it by force,[clxxxi] also the strong man in the wicked world cannot be bound if you are not stronger than the enemy. Jesus also said that, "And I will give unto thee the keys of the kingdom of heaven: and whatsoever thou shalt bind on earth shall be bound in heaven: and whatsoever thou shalt loose on earth shall be loosed in heaven."[clxxxii] There is power in agreement prayers. When two or three pray in Jesus' name, there is deliverance. Therefore, you need prayers. Do not keep quiet over your situations that oppress and possess your peace of mind. Fifth, you must be adherent to holy life. Note this: Prayer without holy life is like driving a car without tyres. Your private life is very important to God. When you sin, you allow devil to add more pain and sorrow to your life. Be ready to surrender your life to Christ and the battle will shift base to God. Your battle is His battle. When you pray believe in your heart that God hears, then you will have victory indeed. Be careful in seeking for spiritual help from where there is no help. Beware of prayer contractors. Prayer is not automatic code that changes God. No! Then, you need to understand what prayer is and what is not.

What prayer is not? Prayer is not cursing of enemies. Prayer is not magical. Prayer is not trade by barter. Prayer is not part time deal with God–It is not only for problem solving. Prayer is not automatic or mechanical. Prayer is not a cover-up. Prayer is not by intellect compositions. Prayer is not a spiritual gift. Prayer is not unto man. Prayer is not contractual.[clxxxiii] Then, what is Prayer? Prayer is communion with God. Prayer is an act of going into God's presence for fellowship. Prayer is bringing God and His resources into our earthly realities. Prayer is drawing out divine resources to influence human reality. Prayer is trusting to entrust our burden to God. Without prayer, our activities are empty. A Christian who lacks the breath of heaven (God's direction and strength) will never last in things of God. A student, who desires lasting solution for any spiritual problems life, must live a life of prayer daily.[clxxxiv] As you pray, you must trust God for solution. Don't be like a woman who is helped by a man inside his car. She enters the car with a load on the head still, despite the comfort she has. She never releases her load for the car to carry. When you pray, trust God that He will care for you and your load. Bible says, "Cast all your care upon Him, for He cares for you–He thinks about you"[clxxxv]Do you ever think that the God who created the whole world is busy thinking about you and your depression? God thinks. He does not act in haste. When He delays answers, He's only waiting for the right time when you will enjoy the blessing at the best. So keep on trusting God for your breakthrough–Do not patronize spiritual contactors; it would be dangerous you did. If a matter is too little to pray about, then it is too little to worry about. Therefore pray over everything as Bible says, "Be anxious for nothing, but in everything by prayer and supplication, with thanksgiving, let your requests be made known to God; and the peace of God, which surpasses all understanding, will guard your hearts and minds through Christ Jesus."[clxxxvi]

Depression ten – Health tussles

Another issue that can cause depression for student is health issue. When there is health there is hope. Many things can hinder students' health. If the mind is sick, the whole body will be sick and vice versa. In chapter three, health negligence was analyzed and it is one of the causes of ill-health for the students in campuses. Others are within the body crises such as sickle cell, diabetes, kidney disease, HIV/AIDS, STD, asthma, cancer, and other numerous diseases. A student with any of these crises will not be able to learn, read, or study as it ought to be.

Some sicknesses are self-inflicted. Why? If a student does not eat at the right time, ulcer is not far away from such student. A student, who is restless and does not sleep well, will suffer migraine, memory loss, high temperature that may open you up to other sickness. A student who cares less about any water – anything is drinkable – and unhygienic food, such student is a close neighbour to typhoid disease. When you sleep without mosquitoes net (at area where mosquitoes dominate the neighborhood), such student will continue to suffer Malaria disease; and if not treated well may lead to Malaria Plus, seizure, dementia (memory loss), etc. A student, who cannot control his /her fashion pursuit and always make up with cancerous creams and cosmetics, may end up with cancer diseases. A student who smokes is in danger of lung diseases, kidney failure, and high blood pressure. A student who enjoys fornication (sexual immorality of all forms) has tendency of contracting HIV type 1 or 2, STD–gonorrhea, syphilis, etc.–hepatitis A, B and C, mouth cancer and others. A student who takes contraceptive pills to stop pregnancy is in danger. The pills will later stop your womb from having children when she needs them and it has tendency to deform your shape and physique.

Sickness and diseases is an agent of depression. You can avoid it. Obey the simple rule of sound health: Precaution is better than cure. Self-medication should be eradicated among students. Do not use contraceptive pills for any reason as unmarried students. Eat balanced diet at the right time. Do not omit your meal for anything. Observe break time during your reading exercises. Engage your body with physical exercise. Do sporting activities. Avoid hard drinks and drugs. Lastly, pray and believe God for sound health. Spiritual thinking will not, of course, guarantee that you will be without sickness, but it definitely can improve your health average. Think health, practice health and pray health for vitality and aliveness. Keep exercising your mind for as you think health, you will be conscious of dos and don'ts of good health. Do you know that only the living and the healthy ones get to the top of their careers? A dream of future without body is as good as dead body without hope of life. Preserve your

health, protect your mind and maintain your relationship with
God.

CHAPTER TEN

LIMITATIONS TO THE MIND OF STUDENT

Limitation one – When you stop reading

Reading is a starter, builder, sustainer and refresher of students' capacity. Mind is open to information through the body gates–senses–and if the gate is open for long without any passage of information, the mind will return to its initial form of idleness. You read to keep mindset right and bright. Being a reader does not only make you a leader but also relevant thinking tank. When you fill your mind with books, you talk sense better than your colleagues and your words will carry weight–making sense to the hearers. However, if you stop to read, what will happen?

- You will begin to experience gradual death intellectually.
- You will become ignorant of what you think you know.
- You will be irrelevant among your colleagues on the field.
- You will have few words to say when others fill the air with wealth of knowledge.
- You will experience scarcity of ideas.
- You will never have opportunity to lead well.
- You will be poor, that is, relevant information for success will be far from you.
- You will be cheated by your mate and juniors.
- You will go down the lane of history.
- You will grow faster than your age. Lack of information makes one aged because you will fall victim of wrong medication, wrong food, loss-oriented business, etc.
- You will not be able to continue easily from when and where you stopped.
- You will lack update.

- Once you stop to read, you will surely exhaust what you know and become obsolete.
- Generations are recognized by their new development in discovery, invention, knowledge and culture. When you stop to read, you will be attached to your past generation alone and be a stranger to the next generation.

Reading empowers the mind. Any negligence to reading shall cause limitations to what your mind can do. Your capacity depends on what your mind can contain. Bible says, "For as a man thinks in his heart, so is he"[clxxxvii], and "A good man out of the good treasure of his heart brings forth that which is good; and an evil man out of the evil treasure of his heart brings forth that which is evil: for of the abundance of the heart his mouth speaks.[clxxxviii] What do you treasure? Is it empty treasury of brain or what? As a student with vibrant brain that can think, read, study, observe and learn, it is a must for you to keep on with books as long as you journey to your reality country of future dream. Don't just read books; read relevant and educating books that will channel you to your dream. A professor who stops to read is equal to an illiterate who has never gone to school. Even after your tertiary education, do not stop reading; it's health to your mind.

Limitation two – When you do it alone
Limitation to the worth of the mind can emerge when you resume the city of one-track throne of knowledge. "I can do ALL THINGS ALONE" is the logo of a student who will soon become irrelevant in the journey of future dreams. There is no island of knowledge. There is what is called Transfer of knowledge. What you know today is given to you by someone. Whatever you have and shared will increase surely. Bible says, "Give and it will be given to you: good measure, pressed down, shaken together, and running over will be put into your bosom. For with the same measure that you use, it will be measured back to you."[clxxxix] You become archaic when you hoard knowledge. What will be the portion of whoever keeps knowledge away from others?

- You will exhaust yours and queue behind others for new ones.
- You can only be a one-time champion and go to archives after.
- You will only know one way of doing it.
- What you share will reproduce in the mind of those who receive the knowledge.
- Your mistakes will be covered when and if you share with others. How? Before you come to stardom, you rehearse with the fellows and finalize your work at home. Suggestions and comments may add excellent grade to your work.
- You will become better professor of the field.

Anyone who keeps to self will not see himself. As a mirror cannot see itself so it shall be. Only the fellow students will see your error for improvement. Team spirit builds invention. I watched a discovery programme on how airbus (airplane) is built.[cxc] The plane was joined together after different companies from different countries worked on the plane. The cabin and the pilot control part were built from Germany, the wings from France while the passengers part from USA. The main company now imported the part for coupling. It was wonderful. If the advanced countries do not monopolize the industry, as a student fill your mind with sharing power and humility to learn from others.

Limitation three – When you ignore God
"The fool has said in his heart, "There is no God.""[cxci] As you journey intellectually, be cautious of atheisms that cancerously eat up the divinity of God in the heart of scholars. There is end to man's knowledge. What you think you know today will surely become archaic because God will not allow anyone to monopolize knowledge and be equal to Him; only God is all in all. He is self-sufficient. He can live without us, but we cannot live without Him. As a student who dreams about tomorrow, you must acknowledge God in your journey. When you ignore God, you ignore relevance. There was a king in the Bible called

Nebuchadnezzar who ignored God in his kingdom. He relied on the knowledge of his astronomers, dream interpreter, witches, sorcerers and administrators. He was proud and God dealt with him. Bible notes the end of the story this was, "The king spoke, saying, "Is not this great Babylon, that I have built for a royal dwelling by my mighty power and for the honor of my majesty?" While the word was still in the king's mouth, a voice fell from heaven: "King Nebuchadnezzar, to you it is spoken: the kingdom has departed from you! And they shall drive you from men, and your dwelling shall be with the beasts of the field. They shall make you eat grass like oxen; and seven times shall pass over you, until you know that the Most High rules in the kingdom of men, and gives it to whomever He chooses." That very hour the word was fulfilled concerning Nebuchadnezzar; he was driven from men and ate grass like oxen; his body was wet with the dew of heaven till his hair had grown like eagles' feathers and his nails like birds' claws. And at the end of the time I, Nebuchadnezzar, lifted my eyes to heaven, and my understanding returned to me; and I blessed the Most High and praised and honored Him who lives forever: For His dominion is an everlasting dominion, And His kingdom is from generation to generation. All the inhabitants of the earth are reputed as nothing; He does according to His will in the army of heaven and among the inhabitants of the earth. No one can restrain His hand or say to Him, "What have you done?" At the same time my reason returned to me, and for the glory of my kingdom, my honor and splendor returned to me. My counselors and nobles resorted to me, I was restored to my kingdom, and excellent majesty was added to me. Now I, Nebuchadnezzar, praise and extol and honor the King of heaven, all of whose works are truth, and His ways justice. And those who walk in pride He is able to put down."[cxcii]

God made everyone, including the students and their learning minds. Anyone who ignores God in learning has ignored Him who created mortal body and graciously breathed in him to live. "Woe to him who strives with his Maker! Let the potsherd strive with the potsherds of the earth! Shall the clay say to him who forms it, 'What are you making?' Or shall your handiwork say, 'He has no hands'?"[cxciii] "Surely you have things turned around! Shall the potter be esteemed as the clay; for shall the thing made say of him who made it, "He did not make me"? Or shall the thing formed say of him who formed it, "He has no understanding"?"[cxciv] Knowledge without God is equal to madness. Man can never comprehend God's existence with this book knowledge. "Have you not known? Have you not heard? The everlasting God, the LORD, The Creator of the ends of the earth, neither faints nor is weary. His understanding is unsearchable."[cxcv] I have some rhetorical questions to ask you. Why do the geniuses die and they do not invent eternal life for their mortal bodies? Why do we bury the geniuses with their brains without being used again by another? Why do we ignore some inventions after years of new inventions? Only God lives forever. Having breath of life and ability to think widely does not equate you with God. Some become atheists, agnostics and free thinkers. Too much of knowledge will not allow a scholar to acknowledge and glorify God. But Daniel did. "Then the secret was revealed to Daniel in a night vision. So Daniel blessed the God of heaven. Daniel answered and said: "Blessed be the name of God forever and ever, For wisdom and might are His.""[cxcvi] Knowledge without wisdom and understanding is irrelevant. "From where then does wisdom come? And where is the place of understanding? 'Behold, the fear of the Lord, that is wisdom, and to depart from evil is understanding.'"[cxcvii] "Let not the wise man (student) glory in his wisdom, let not the mighty man (scholar) glory in his might, nor let the rich man (genius) glory in his riches; but let him who glories glory in this, that he understands and knows Me (God)…"[cxcviii]

Nevertheless, how can a student ignore God in studentship? Is it really possible? Yes!

- When you build confidence in your capacity alone.
- When you talk rudely and proudly about your achievement as your effort.

- When you do not pray to God as student.
- When you begin to use your mind to assume inexistence of God.
- When you deny the input of God in your career.
- When you look down on anyone below your capacity.
- When you ridicule things of God with your knowledge.

A student with sound mind will love and pray to God for help. Remember, He created your brain to think right. Have you ever considered other fellows who are mad, mentally retarded, memory loss victim, head tumor patient or student with head injury? What will be their hope for tomorrow's dream as you also pursue? Then, never ignore God in your life, schooling, and career pursuit.

Limitation four – When you live on rugged ambition, not on purpose

Ambition[cxcix] is a desire for success; a strong feeling of wanting to be successful in life and achieve great things. The desire is ardent, strong, and earnest. It makes a student to run after power, honour, achievement, wealth and distinctive attainment. Ambition runs round the veins of an ambitious student to have something done within a space of time. Ambition is like downpour rain that only goes on to reach the earth–the target point, or like vehicle that loses control. Ambition is powerful and it can drive any crazy. However, whenever a student fills his with ambition, the race will be tough and rigorous without counting the loss or gain on the road. Purpose is good for student. Purpose is from the beginning of life to the end. It runs steady and progressive without a crazy push to get at all cost. Purpose comes before any action, it controls at the middle and end to evaluate the action. Purpose is under control while ambition makes a student ruthless. How? Some students want success at all cost to keep their ambition going and will not mind to commit malpractices, impersonation, sex payback for the lecturers, looking for miracle centers, etc. Purposeful students will seek to protect their reputation but ambitious student is success-drunk with ruthless actions–bribery, cultism, killing, etc. Some students after achieving their ambition, they have no respect for moral life. Like a medical doctor who knows the dignity of the work and still womanize, smoke and drink alcoholic, though a bright and brilliant doctor. He wants ambition but throws away purpose for living. Purpose is God's driven but ambition is self-driven. Purposeful student will handle failure as part of life and move on but ambitious students will do anything to stop failure. Ambitious students have lack of contentment. You become what you dream to fulfill purpose for living–helping the poor, standing for justice–however, if all you live for is to get degree and recognition, you have wasted your studentship.

How does ambition limit your mind as student?

- Ambition limits your mind to what you think you know.
- Ambition will deny you link with other fellows that do not study or operate what you are doing.
- It makes one redundant after the ambition is achieved – nothing more, nothing less.
- It grows the body older because you would have wasted all energy on just one thing. Purpose outlives the purposeful student - it follows in different dimensions.
- Your mind will not work well again as if there is no other useful thing to do.

When you plant your dream in ambitious soil, you will only be relevant during the height of the ambition and after that you become irrelevant. Think wide. Think purposefully. Think beyond your age. Do not restrict your thought on what your generation alone will benefit from. Exercise your mind with great dream of purpose. Do you even know why you are living? Do you know what you are born to solve? Did you choose your course on purpose or proud ambition? Have you ever seen the traces of your existence in your daily living? If yes, maintain and keep it alive. If no, seek the face of your Creator who knows why you exist. Bible says what God plans about your purpose. "For I know the thoughts that I think toward you, says the LORD, thoughts of *peace* and not of evil, *to give you a future and a hope.*"[cc] "There is hope in your future, says the LORD..."[cci] If you have not given your life to Christ, you are still playing around ambitious life that may be ruthless, dangerous and selfish. Only in Christ you can find meaning to life. Try Him today.

Limitation five – When you stop to dream, to live on the past

Dream must be continuous to be sustained. You dream to see the end with joy every day. It is an inner drive that keeps great dreamers on. Joseph had dreams and kept dreaming even in the difficult time of his life. "Now Joseph had a dream, and he told it to his brothers; and they hated him even more."[ccii] He did not stop to dream even when the envious brothers threatened him. "Then he dreamed still another dream and told it to his brothers..."[cciii] If you were Joseph will you tell envious people again? The journey of future is far but close to the mind of student. As we dream, we fail, fall, and faint, yet we fire on. We live to convert today to past and tomorrow to today. If you keep seeing the envious people of the past, past mistakes, past embarrassment, etc., it will discourage your mind to dream on. When you stop to dream and you will live on the past.

Limitation six – When health maintenance is ignored

Good health is the author of sound mind. Students who want achievement of dream will maintain their health. Chapter three and nine of this book address issue of health (health negligence and health tussle), you can read again to avoid limitation along the way to your dream.

Limitation seven – When love of sex and money controls the mind

Mind and sex life are friends and foes. Your approach will determine the position of the mind. In chapter eight of this book where distractions of the mind of student were discussed; issue of sexual immorality was reviewed exclusively. Sex is mind-wired. No man will have aroused body without the mind. If you ignore a bad picture (nude lady) at first-sight, it will not register the image in your mind. It is necessary for a purposeful student to guide against every way that immorality passes to the mind. You need to question what your eyes are passionate of seeing – nude media board, nude magazine, nude lady on the campus, etc. It will only deposit sand of distractions and when you need to regurgitate what you have learnt in the school, sex will come alive in your mind. Another limiting factor to mind is money matter. Money answers many things but love of money kills. When you devote your mind to money, you will lose focus fast. Many inventors produced great inventions to be wealthy immediately but love of money choked the dream. Some people bought the idea, formula and principle with money – countable money- and left the inventors empty till date. Let the love of your people and community, and your purpose fill your mind to do more. Money will finish but your good name will last. When love for money grows, dishonesty will scale in–it is from the mind.

My dear reader, the mind within you is loaded with great ideas and opportunities. However, your acts and attitude can limit its power. Student with mission will not allow limiting factors earlier discussed to stop the dream-driven mind of yours. The sky is the beginning of your purposeful touch of love in this world. Catch you there.

CHAPTER ELEVEN
ABOUT TO LAUNCH OUT

"On your mark, set, go!" is the instruction to the athletes. About to launch what your mind has in stock, you need to understand some principles that will guide you on the track as scholar in embryo. An adage says, "Look before you leap." It is better to prepare well before acting than to act unprepared. Preparation may last many years, months and days; it doesn't matter. Your time of glory cannot be used by anyone or given to another person. Wait patiently before you launch out. I know you have skills, power, inspiration, artistic ability, creativity and so on; you need to gather momentum before you face the stardom. May God prepare you well with everything you need. Amen. A rocket passes through a swift velocity to discharge into the space. These are tested guides that will prepare your mind for higher ground.

PREPARATION ONE: DREAM SMARTLY

As you dream to change Africa and the world, let your dream be smart.[cciv] How? SMART is an acronym standing for specific, measurable, attainable, realistic and time-bound. **Dream must be specific**–i.e. what do you think you are capable of solving, propounding, providing, discovering, inventing, promoting or formulating? Give it any name. Where and when do you want to fulfill the dream? How will you fulfill the dream? Be specific on black and white. **Dream must be measurable** – it needs a control measure to check whether you are on the track or not. Dream may fade or miss track to another route. If the dream has measure, you will know. Do you dream of inventing or discovering drugs for Africa use at tender age within this discouraging economy and your basic education? Is it really possible? Do you have access to materials and men at this age? Then, let your dream grow with measure of time. If you are planting for a year, sow rice; if you are planting for a decade, plant trees; if you are planning for lifetime, educate yourself and people.[ccv] Schooling grows dream better.

Dream must be attainable. If you dream to formulate economic principle to save Africa from economic meltdown, then you must know more about core economics. But if you only study applied science without social science, such dream is not attainable. How many hours do you spend for reading? One hour to two hours per week? Dream to discover Ebola vaccines may not be attainable because you need days of sleepless research. Do you watch discovery programmes or Africa Magic channel often? If you want to know more in technological inventions, you reduce leisure time for lecture and reading. **Dream must be realistic –** genuine. Your sincerity on the dream is very important. Do you desire to produce the next car design because you saw the glamour and popularity of Aliyu Jelani of Sokoto State on TV who designed Chevrolet Volt for US? Or you dream to be a newscaster in order to display your eloquence and beauty? This kind of dream is not realistic – it has not discovered a problem to solve yet. Dreamers are problem solvers. **Dream must be time-bound** – when do you think you will be ripe to get the dream completed? All these facts about dream preparation will smartly prepare your dream for stardom.

PREPARATION TWO: KNOW THE PROBLEMS

Do you have a problem? Be sincere with the answer. Yes! No! Which one? Inventors have load of problems to solve. No problem, no dream of solution. Vincent Norman congratulated a fellow[ccvi] because he had problems. What a surprising greeting! Everyone lives daily to either solve one problem or create another one. Mothers in the kitchen solve problems of hunger by providing food; this solution causes the children to go to toilet to defecate because of digestion. This problem is solved by the building engineers who install and fix toilet system. An inventor produces a gadget like phone. This same phone will have another problem of installation and re-fixing of error that will need another thinker/solver of problems. Do you think solution or you just consume someone's solution only? Prepare to identify a problem that you are studying to solve. Why do you go to school? Are you burdened to help some people that are victims of rape, injustice, cheat, and unlawful discrimination? Then, you will go for Law and specialize later either on civil Law, human right Law, or criminal law. Maybe you discovered maternity death rate last time you visited hospital and it pierced your mind because only a few doctors were on duty. Then, you will study Medicine and later go on to specialize on gynecology. Know the problem to solve now than later.

PREPARATION THREE: PLAN FOR THE EXPECTED PRODUCT OF THE DREAM

Dream is like a pregnancy that cannot be purely predetermined what it will bring forth at the delivery date but you can plan ahead for the expected product–solution. Dream needs planning. It all starts from primary school to secondary and later to tertiary institution. Do you still move on with the dream of your tender age as you climb the ladder of learning? If yes, plan to hold it on. Some students have conflict with parents on the career to study. Career is the wheel of your dream. Some parents even throw away the dream because of reasons best known to them. My reader, you can still have the dream. How? Do not fight back. Do not insult your parents. Do not say "They hate me", "They are not my good parents", or "They are wishing me evil". Be calm and be reasonable with their choice of career for you. God uses parents to guide their children. Seek professional advice from your teacher, school counsellor or anyone on the class of your dream. Show your passion and love for the career through your inventions, discoveries, habitual reading, comments, discussions, kind of programmes you attend, and relationships at home and in the school. Study hard–this is a crystal clear measure that can vindicate you. Prove your choice of career through good results in the school. Provide materials that can educate your parent about the career – the good, the bad (that are manageable) and the ugly. Re-table the career issue with your parent again when they are happy with you. Pray at all times over the issue that God should guide your parents to lead you aright.[ccvii] Keep planning daily to sustain the dream. Watch documentaries that promote keenness for the dream. Again read and study extensively. Build your knowledge on the fundamental of the dream. Gather whatever resources that can help you to get going. Attend seminars and workshops of your dream. Keep record of facts and principles you learn daily for tomorrow's usage. Keep planning, it may last for years.

PREPARATION FOUR: DEAL WITH IMPOSSIBILITIES

Impossibility is a strong odd word in the English language dictionary but not in the dictionary of the student's mind. Great inventors and discoverers faced trapping-net of impossibilities, but they broke through with total determination in God and in their best abilities. Bible confidently says to me, "I can do all things through Christ who strengthens me."[ccviii] Problem is only impossible to be solved at a glance. All you need is to approach the impossibility with mind of possibility. Do you have any examination to write? Face it with faith and confidence. Impossibility cases push away students from trying. There is no crime in trying. Develop strong muscle of possibility in your mind before you reach the point of no return in your dream. Thomas Edison invented numerous useful devices, including a practical electric light bulb and the phonograph when he refused defeat; he tried again, he got another invention.[ccix] Abraham Lincoln refused to see US presidency as impossibility. President Mohammadu Buhari tried three times and kept trying until the word 'impossibility' disappeared in his mind. Deal with it now before you start to view stardom as inheritance of other students. You can do it if you think you can as Vincent Norman used to say. However, friends and parents may come with experiential advice of impossibility, do not lose heart. Try and keep trying, you will get it one day.

PREPARATION FIVE: HOW TO GET AND MAKE IDEAS WORK

Ideas build dreams daily. Ideas are God's blessing in man. When He breathed in man, ideas found a resting abode in man's mind. No one taught Adam how to tend the garden or name the animals. Great ideas are in you. Only serious minded student will retrieve them. Idea reframes and restructures dreams. Geniuses do not play away with ideas. First, write down on paper your three greatest dreams, numbering them one, two, three. Look at this list every day. Second, spend time every day analyzing and studying your dream–invention, discovery, formula, theory, solution, etc. Do this every day, every month and yearly, in few years you will get closer to your dream than when you first started. Third, spend one hour each day with a white sheet of paper in front of you and write down every idea you can think of.[ccx] You will get surprising ideas that will improve your studies, pursuit and dream. Ideas are locked up in books. Read books. Put down each and every concept or notion that occurs to you – good, bad, or indifferent - practical or not – obvious or not – all ideas. Have lots of ideas and later judge the validity for your dream. They are all in your disposal.

PREPARATION SIX: SAFETY FIRST IS NOT THE MOTTO OF RISK-TAKER

Dream to the top goes with risk. Every risk-taker has place on the top seat. Why? They attempted what others ran away from. Their dreams are beyond oral confession. They took steps that lead to the future right away. Have you ever attempted any professional examination? Do you attempt to design or produce anything close to your dream? Risk is everything. Michael Catt also notes the statement that 'safety is not the first thought of risk taker.'[ccxi] "If I perish, I perish" as used in the Bible is the language of risk-taker that dreams a change. The risk-takers give 'one' that they have for 'all.' They sacrifice their pleasure to read, study, discover, and stand out just only to get solution that will save lives in Africa and beyond. Esther practiced 'One-Out-of-One' principle because she loved God and her Jewish people. She dreamt redemption of her people. She concluded to waste her life to save the generation of Jew and to keep on track–the redemptive plan of God through the Jews. Remember, she got to the throne as queen by privilege. She had earlier suffered from poverty and death of her parent. Yet she did not see the opportunity as "mine", but she saw "for all."[ccxii] Being genius is not for you and your family alone; it's for the whole world. Africa lacks risk-takers; that is why we suffer new development in all sectors. No one is ready to bell the cat of newness. Few that tried were discouraged by the corruption of our leaders; these few ones prefer living abroad than being marginalized by the political propagandists.

God has children like Esther in places of authority that can stand for the truth and save the situation of our nation, but complacency, pressure of wealth accumulation, advice of bad friends and relatives, and selfishness, could not. They have eaten accursed food of corruption and cannot boldly stand for God's way. Can God trust you with wealth, discovery, invention, power and authority so that you will fit in into His divine agenda? Esther declared her manifesto for God's will. "Go, gather together all the Jews who are in Susa, and fast for me. Do not eat or drink for three days, night or day. I and my maids will fast as you do. When this is done, I will go to the king, even though it is against the law. And if I perish, I perish."[ccxiii] Students of courage make way where there is no way. We need to break out of the box and drop the baggage. Boxes are designed for storage and shoes, not students with dreams.[ccxiv] It is time to put on the shoe of faith and take an incredible journey with God to save our dying world.

PREPARATION SEVEN: SHIFT FROM COMFORT ZONE
Student who places high value on pleasure and comfort will not achieve his/her dreams. Leisure and lecture time must be separated and defined. Comfort from friendship, partying, lovemaking, watching of seasonal movies, etc. cannot prepare you for the dream. Comfort zone is not the appropriate zone for dreamers. Joseph was at comfort with his father but God allowed discomfort through his envious brother and he got relocated to zone of the champion. Dream attracts discomforts just to keep you alive for your dream.

Like an eagle you have to demonstrate or model the behaviour you expect. The eagle knows the way and shows the way. He also develops the young eaglet. He will not let his offspring lie around, eating and getting lazy.[ccxv] Eagle pushes the eaglet out of his comfort zone. During the time of training the young ones to fly, the mother eagle throws the eaglets out of the nest and because they are scared, they jump back into the nest. Next she throws them out and then takes off the soft layers of the nest, leaving the thorns bare. When the scared eaglets jump into the nest again, thorns puncture them. Screaming and bleeding, they jump out again, this time wondering why the mother and father who love them so much are torturing them. Next, mother eagle pushes them off the cliff into the air. As they scream in fear, father eagle flies out and picks them up on his back before they fall too far, and brings them back to the cliff. This goes on for some times until they start flapping their wings. They get excited at this new found knowledge that they can fly and not fall at such a fast rate. The father and mother eagles support them with their wings.[ccxvi] If you are over-pampered with comfort, you will not value top seat. Why? It is for the great individuals who are trained, disciplined and cultured with discomfort in order to value human lives that suffer discomfort with appropriate helping hands. Our leaders were born with silver-spoons. They do not know our plight. Keep your dream to save helpless children of this generation.

If your parents are like Moses' parent who worked courageously and placed Moses out to a flowing river, you are closer to the dream. Many students have lost their dreams because of the pampering lifestyle of their parents. They make them dependent of all comfort. They cannot even think for themselves. You need to shift away from comfort zone in order to achieve your dream. How many hours do spend for reading? Do you visit library for more research? Do you travel to get more information? Do you join group discussion with others? Or you only read at will when there is no movie to watch or no snacks to eat or no party to go? Students with mind of great dreams will shift away from comfort zone as they prepare to launch out great impact in their regeneration.

PREPARATION EIGHT: THE HIGHER YOU CLIMB THE FEWER THE CHOICES YOU HAVE

As the road narrows, the closer you get to the top. Decisions have to be made. As students, the choices are between good, better and best.[ccxvii] When you were in primary school, the choices were many. As you move, the opportunities also come around you for better choice. The dream of future must keep on progressively with better choice. Prepare for the best. Whenever an inventor fails a trial-test, he tries again for better performance. No one competes in sports with a good point and still dream to remain on the past point. He/she will aspire to get better. Students get better as they read, study, aspire, get motivated and develop their dreams. You climb ladders every time you dream great. When you climb a ladder of great dreams, make sure the ladder is leaning against the right building to avoid sudden fall. Some students lean on parental status, lecturers' promises, political propagandist' influences or a naughty way of achievement, to accomplish their dreams. They can but will fail you. One of the very worst uses of time and opportunity of studentship is to do something very well that need not to be done at all. This is purely abuse of lifetime. When you engage your mind on malpractice with all energy, you are tailoring your mind to futility. Do you know that malpractice has a penalty backed up with Law? According to Annual Newsletter of JAMB 2014, it noted that "The examination malpractice shall be prosecuted with the full weight of the provisions of examination malpractice, Decree No.33 of 1999."[ccxviii] You may say Nigerian law has teeth but cannot bite. Yes, you are correct. But, you have not done it where it will bite you and maybe it is your own time that it will bite harder. If you engage yourself with this evil and you are caught, shame, embarrassment, imprisonment and loss of passion for your dream will push you down the ladder.

Again, remember you are climbing; strength and time also go with the height. You do not waste time on a stage, unless the strength and time will run out. The days used for wrong assignment or careless failure cannot be regained even after doing the right. And taking actions without thinking through at the crucial time of studentship is a prime source of pitfalls. To avoid pitfalls of moving from 'best' to 'good' and 'good' to 'worst', planning is incontrovertible and indispensable, i.e. planning of your strength within the days when the mind is still very potent.

PREPARATION NINE: YOUR ACTION WILL GIVE OTHERS COURAGE

A rat that bells the cat safely has bellowed the air with courage for others. There are millions of students who had lost courage for schooling and life's usefulness due to the failure of some people in their areas. Let me say this: one of the greatest qualities of a dream is the contagious power it has on like-minded people. Every student wants to be a doctor because of Ben Carson, a renowned and successful neurosurgeon. Hear this again: If you fail, they fail. If you win, they win. Have you ever thought of others who looked forward to you for inspiration and motivation for life? Joshua's courage gave others courage. His courage gave the priest courage to lead and step into a river at flood stage. Lloyd John Ogilvie, in his book, *Lord of the Impossible*, describes the scene: the Lord of the impossible had decided to make his miracle depended on the priest getting their feet wet. One step farther and your feet will get wet. There was no turning back. God and the people depended on them."[ccxix] When you attempt greatness, your siblings, school juniors, colleagues and friends will jump into the deep with you and be wet altogether. Your excellent results will surely provoke brilliance among other students. Take the risk of doing what others are not doing. Read, read and read. Daily look at the inscription of best podium you dreamt and never negotiate with failure. Dawson Trottman said, "Think! You can do a lot more than you realize."[ccxx] I can see potentials becoming reality in students of today. I remember hearing John Madden say, "Potential means you haven't done it yet." Joshua realized his potential. Have you begun to realize yours? Joshua understood potential is only realized when there is preparation.[ccxxi] As you prepare to launch out, prepare your mind to think. Prepare your heart to believe God. Then, prepare your mind again to carry out the dream from good to best; others you can never think of, will pick interest in excellence. We must stop heroic celebration of the past heroes. I challenge you to be the next hero that will raise new heroes.

PREPARATION TEN: WORK AS IF ALL DEPENDS ON YOU AND THEN TRUST GOD

Spurgeon said, "The best and wisest thing in the world is to work as if all depended upon you, and then trust in God, knowing that all depend on Him".[ccxxii] God created heavens and earth for five days. He left all for improvement that would come from His creature, man. The preparation to launch out starts from your selfless effort as you read wide, develops ideas and facts, invent smaller devices, write stories, design creatively and so on. The idle hands are liabilities to the body. Work and faith go together. As you work as student, you pray as a believer in God because all still depend on Him. Do not be like a girl I met when I went for an examination in one town. This girl did not prepare at all for this examination. She had faith in the teachers who had collected money for malpractice. Unfortunately, the hall was filled up with external supervisors, policemen and workers from the Ministry of Education for the mathematics paper. All effort preplanned with the teachers failed woefully. During the break time, I was at a corner reading for the next paper. I had the conversation of another girl with this unfortunate girl. She said, "Why are you crying? Is it because of this paper? Bible says 'we should not worry.' I will give you an advice, "Go for fervent and 'holyghostlistic' seven (7) days fasting and prayers, the result of this paper will be A1""[ccxxiii] I laughed and still pity their ignorance. God is not a magician. He will never work out what you have no input there. Bible says, "Do you see a man (student) who excels in his work? He will stand before kings; He will not stand before unknown men."[ccxxiv] Jesus said, "I must work the works of Him who sent Me while it is day; the night is coming when no one can work."[ccxxv] Even Jesus worked and prayed. As you work as students, do not forget the place of God, "For it is God who works in you both to will and to do for His good pleasure."[ccxxvi] If you are able to prepare well before launching out, the sky will become your abode of accomplishments. And a good preparation without the author of success, Jesus Christ, is equal to nothing. If you have not accepted Him as Saviour and Lord, you cannot do all things. He is waiting for your decision now.

CHAPTER TWELVE

EXPECTED PRODUCTS FROM THE MIND OF STUDENT –
GIVE BIRTH TO AFRICA'S SOLUTION

Where is Africa on the map of developed continents? Why does Africa still struggle to rise? Africa, as a continent of the black and the dark in complexion, has passed through a lot of hatred, dehumanization, prejudices and treatment like the inferior even at the level of gospel propagation by the white. Africa is nations of subject of debate by the theologians and scholars on her existence and resources. This is Africa in its immensity, the second continent in size on the globe.[ccxxvii] Africa is a land of chilly plateaus, snow-clad mountains, extensive jungles, humid coastal regions and hot sands as Jelani Aliyu,[ccxxviii] an African inventor, proudly describes as his fatherland.[ccxxix] There is, of course, rich soil in abundance in many parts of Africa and enough rainfall to make everything grow profusely. Sometimes there is altogether too much rain so that tropical rain forest takes over. However, poor soil and dry climate leave millions of hard-working people undernourished and poverty stricken. The riches of the mineral resources, found in amazing varieties and amounts all over the continent, supply the world with the economic stability of gold, the fused strength of manganese with iron, the beauty and hard cutting edge of diamonds, the healing power of radium[ccxxx] and crude oil in excess for refining overseas.

Many Africans live from hand to mouth in bare existence and know only a dreary substandard life, but not all the people live like this. Africa is a continent of exploding populations and areas of rapid social change. In spite of changes already made, millions of Africans awaits health, education, and a community fellowship.[ccxxxi] Booth also notes that Africa stands out as the last major area of the world where colonialism continues. More than colonialism, however, is involved. The excessive use by the white man of Africa's resources is a violation of human freedom.[ccxxxii] Africa is poor and rich. Why this oxymoron? We have what it takes to transform our world. We have human resources in which you are one of them. We have material resources in the valleys, mountains, plains and forest. We have methodology for development on papers that lie idle in the morgue of libraries of our tertiary institutions. We are lenient but no impacts. We argue policy. We consume finished products. We do not embrace Africa-made goods. We make Africa poor. I feel sad to see millions of Africa migrating to other continents in order to seek greener pastures for their futures through Morocco to Spain and some died on the blue se unburied. In Africa, future is blinking because of our leaders who have the future in their hands and are careless about us. Sometime we argued that colonial masters caused our woes. What about now, after ten decades? We are in charge of our destiny, yet we cannot vouch of Africa-made products, ideas, theories, inventions, that are saleable in other continents. I write this book to stir up holy and inventive anger in the sleeping African youth and students that have dreams of our solutions, to stand out for revitalization of this continent.

African countries, especially Nigeria, have able students who can successfully provide answers to our daily problems. Problem of economical decadence, problem of non-commercialized scientific discoveries, problem of leadership, problem of sustainable research and development, problem of technological transfer and contextualization, etc. need to be dealt with. Our problems have nothing to do with our make as black; it is our state of mind that is faulty. That is what the white men saw in us during colonization. The colour of skin has nothing to do with underdevelopment in Africa. Though Africa has dark world of power and evil, but it is not limited to Africa alone. Also the cultural symbols, instruments and heritage in music and art, which crossed the Atlantic, made the white to observe in their perspective that African are dark in knowledge, social expression and theology.[ccxxxiii]

Malaysia was an under-developed country many years ago. There was a deliberate state of emergency against poverty. Richard Ulack notes that the economy of Malaysia once relied principally on the production of raw materials for export, most importantly petroleum, natural rubber, tin, palm oil, and timber. After Malaysia gained independence in 1957, however, the development of the manufacturing sector took priority. From the mid-1970s to mid-1990s Malaysia had one of the world's fastest-growing economies, mainly due to rapid industrialization. In 1991 the Malaysian government launched the ambitious "Vision 2020" programme, which envisions Malaysia attaining the status of a developed nation by 2020. Toward this goal, the government has invested heavily in modernizing the infrastructure of the Kuala Lumpur metropolitan area. The modernization is designed to propel Malaysia into the digital age and position it as a hub for high-technology businesses in Southeast Asia.[ccxxxiv]

At this point, the student who has the mind for sustainable change and still on track to the reality of dream should consider the expected products that will move Africa and Nigeria forward.

EXPECTED PRODUCT ONE – SCHOLARSHIP WITH PROACTIVE ENTREPRENEURSHIP

In our tertiary institutions, the purpose of academics is to build and develop scholarship in the students in the area of their interest. Nigeria has millions of scholars that have books, theories, dissertation and thesis to their credit in the schools' library. They have discovered and rediscovered facts on their disciplines but have not remarkably linked them to physical means that an average Nigerian can enjoy for livelihood. I wondered why Ebola disease could last months in Nigeria when we have premier universities where researches go on almost every academic session. The economic situation of Nigeria is dying and the professors of economics have never come forth with visible and viable tools to solve the problem. President Buhari through his spokesman said, "I challenged Nigerian economist to tell me what benefits Nigeria has earned from the devaluation so far... I have to reluctantly give up because the so-called Nigeria economist come and talk things to me and when I raised issues, they talk over my head instead of inside my head."[ccxxxv] It means the so-called scholars talked jargons instead of meaningful and proactive solution that even the kindergarten pupils can easily understand and apply. Students who cannot explain their disciplines as simple as ABC may not be able to get the dream realized. There is need for simplicity in scholarship.

Mention is not enough. Tesla invented the electric power we use, but he struggled to get it out to people. You have to combine both things: invention and innovation focus, plans the company that can commercialize things and get them to people – Larry Page

The expected products for Africa development are academics knowledge that has quantifiable results in the economic, social and health life of the citizens. It should convert research into innovation with commercial potential and intention. The projects at the end of each academic pursuit and the papers presented to earn doctorate degree should be bellowed with life that will change the system of Africa for development. I have this advice for students. Do not write long essay project only to earn grade or to impress your supervisor, but do all the best to gather facts, principles and way out that can be applied to make life better for the citizenry. 'Copy and paste' attitude towards final papers is a cheat on your ability as student. What you copied is someone's idea. You can research and develop papers with possible solution for Nigerians. Before a scholastic work begins, there should be a problem on the table to solve. I mean in the mind of the student. Going to school should reduce our communal problems; not to add to problem of unemployment. Do not finish tertiary institution with the mind of seeking for white and blue collar job. Remember, it is someone's idea. You can create one.

In 2012, I met a group of graduates in Ilorin who refused to add up to numbers of job seekers in Nigeria Street. They innovatively started a firm that designs and builds websites, portal for schools, and mobile apps development. They pay themselves as the firm grows. They are graduates of Computer Science from

University of Ilorin. They refuse to develop scholarship only; their business idea is academically sandwiched with entrepreneurial innovation.[ccxxxvi] If all students will think like *Jelani Aliyu* (designer of Chevrolet volt); *Dimeji Falana* (who designed apps for schools – EDVES - and apps for food vendors – HOJAH); *Seyi Oyesola* (the co-invention of CompactOR or the "Hospital in a Box"); and others, you would study hard to earn living from your career and also to be a blessing to Nigeria. Why? Your products will add value to Nigeria's economy in exporting of inventions to other countries, reduce unemployment and it will build industrialization in Africa. Let check through the biography of these great heroes of invention that converted academics knowledge to commercialized innovation.

Jelani Aliyu was born in Kaduna State, Nigeria in 1966. He originates from Sokoto State, Nigeria and earned an associate degree in Architecture from Birnin Kebbi Polytechnic in 1988. Upon graduation from the Polytechnic, Jelani worked at the Ministry of Works, Sokoto before pursuing additional education in the United States. He graduated in 1994 with a degree in Automobile Design from the College for Creative Studies, Detroit, Michigan and was hired by General Motors. Jelani Aliyu is credited with designing General Motors' leading auto brand, Chevrolet Volt.[ccxxxvii]

Dimeji Falana was born in Ikire, Osun State, Nigeria. He graduated from University of Ilorin with good grade in Computer Science. He has this to his credit, development of government and private schools websites and portals, invention of mobile apps called EDVES for proper school management at primary, secondary and tertiary institution levels and also HOJAH, apps that connects food vendors to customers without physical contacts. It runs nationwide and in some Africa countries.[ccxxxviii]

Since year 2000, **Shehu Balami**, a Nigerian Engineer has been involved in designing rockets. He is a graduate of Mechanical Engineering from the Federal University of Technology (FUT), Minna, Niger State. He has produced two solid fuel rockets which were launched along the new Kaduna Millennium City Road in Kaduna State. In 2008, with the support of his friends and family members, he was able to build his first rocket which he later modified in 2011. The solid-fuel rocket was produced under the auspices of the Movement for the Propagation of Science and Technology in Nigeria. He produced the two rockets with 100 per cent local materials at an approximate cost of 30,000 naira each (approximately 190 dollars).[ccxxxix]

Our future growth relies on competitiveness and innovation, skills and productivity… and these in turn rely on the education of our people – Julia Gillard

These biographies include just a few of our talented youths who had their first degree in Nigeria and still innovatively invented great things. You can do the same. Do not wait for job; create one as you read and study in your school. Be futuristic in your approach. These one never spoil their mind with distractions of the school. They focused on the future and kept dreaming. Nigeria and Africa need people like this; people who will showcase the value of blackness in inventions. On the hall of fame list of inventors in Nigeria and beyond, will your name be there?

As you learn in the school, think about these opportunities of knowledge-based economy such as biotechnology, advanced materials production, communication, entertainment, mobile technology, etc. In India, the economy jumped up because the country converted knowledge to entrepreneurship-based economy. The country developed the aspect of software development. From a LinkedIn Pulse of Ruturai Trivedi, a business Manager for Web and Mobile Apps, and Ecommerce, I discovered why many nations still outsource for software from India. India is a talent-rich country like Nigeria. India exports software to 95 countries around the world. India enjoys the confidence of global corporations; 82% of US companies ranked India as their first choice for software outsourcing.[ccxl] Bill Clinton applauds India's brainpower, he says, "Indian-Americans run more than 750 companies in America's Silicon Valley. You liberated your markets and now you have one of the ten fastest growing economies in the world."[ccxli] Bill Gate says, "India is an IT superpower: strikes strategic alliances with Wipro and Infosys to develop applications on the .Net platform."[ccxlii] IT is the major thrust area for the Government of India. As for Nigeria, your discipline (career) can place us on the high platform with advanced countries if you study to invent new ideas, only when you engage your mind now.

EXPECTED PRODUCTS TWO – DYNAMIC AND CORRUPT-FREE LEADERSHIP

Africa is in need. We have men but we do not have leaders. We have men of great inventions and discoveries but the available leaders are consumers and discouragers of great exploit. I felt bad when I see the blessing of God on the black race whether in Africa or America–black singers, black actors, black soldiers, black engineers, black doctors, etc. We have access to in-depth knowledge of science, technology, literature, music, scholarship, health, etc. Yet we cannot boast of Nigeria-made products that can compete in the world class product level. We can but our leaders do not. The worth and value of a leader is what he/she will embrace. When our democratic journey started in 1999, the so-called leaders who wanted to lead us emerged with fake certificate of schools they never attended, just to impress the masses and imposed themselves unduly. One of them is Salisu Buhari who is a former Speaker of the House of Representatives in Nigeria and was impeached from office in 1999 after it was discovered that he forged his university certificate from Toronto University. [ccxliii] How will you expect free and fair leadership for him/her who got power through corruption? How will they place value on education that did not have? Chinedu Arizona-Ogwu, a Nigeria-America online blogger, adds that for fifty years now the Nigerian politicians have left education to decay. An educational system in Nigeria is all about providing credentials, not skills and integrity, to their graduates. Labour markets also reward credentials rather than skills and integrity.[ccxliv] All students and graduates want to rule without due scepter of leadership. It is only in Africa that the blind lead the seeing.

You and I know the value of schooling for average of 16 years. They do not know because they have power to rule the masses at their backyard through age-long god-fatherism and nepotism. We cannot change this evil with mere protest or rioting or silence, unless we desire change through our selfless reading, learning, discovering, inventing, developing and formulating of ideas that will overrule their propaganda in the next generation. Do not stop your dream. Your determination will keep you on track and prepared when the time-bomb of revolution will suddenly hit Nigeria leadership and scatter the cabalism. Only the prepared ones will take over.

It's becoming a reality that corruption has come to replace our national anthem. We hear and read it every day on TV, radio, newspaper, online pages, etc. The system of governance is tired of corrupt practices and corrupt officers who had sworn allegiance to their belly and bank account that all money at their disposal will be stolen. These people are gradually maiming and killing education and schooling. However, some students may think odd - what is the essence of going to school and get certificate that will never get allowances that corrupt leaders get per day? It is sad and heart-stricken. In 1996, I was able to listen to a dialogue of two boys who had decided to participate in corruption process in Nigeria. One said, "I will steal money when I grow up because the national cake is for all of us", other boy responded, "I too will steal to buy cars, houses and be fine, because national cake is not for some people." Unfortunately, these children were between 4 to 5 years old. If this seed of corruption has been planted at this age, what will be the future of Nigeria and beyond the shore?

A leader that will save Nigeria, the expected product, will grow with integrity proven from his/her community, school environment and religious setup. Integrity is not reputation. It is a lifestyle. Reputation can be earned and be bought through being a philanthropist, activists, etc. What you are is different from what people call you. From the school days, your interaction with other colleagues is a test on what your future and dream holds. Did you lead when you were in primary school? Did you handle money matter successfully in your secondary school days? Did the school recommend you for right living or group you with bad boys of the session? Change for integrity doesn't come up suddenly. You build it over years. I was opportune to witness the evil of politics in tertiary institution. In 2000, at Osun State Polytechnic, Iree, we had Student Union Government election and it was fatal and deadly. The presidential candidates sought for lives of one another through diabolical means. Some candidates quitted to save their lives. At the end, one emerged as the president with trust that he would serve the students. Unfortunately, the president and the financial secretary printed extra receipts to collect undocumented dues from students. They acquired lands, grinding machines, motorcycles and electronics. I was sorry for Nigerian politics because these souls would one day go for a senatorial district seat and still repeat the history. This matter of corruption is from the mind. You can erase the thought and be firm to stand for truth.

A leader who is politically drunk for power will do and undo anything. Power tends to corrupt, and absolute power corrupts absolutely.[ccxlv] Unlimited power is apt to corrupt the minds of those who possess it.[ccxlvi] Students that dream future should do with ease and steady pace. Note this: what you are able to get from school, or make yourself in the process will grant you power. Which power? - Power to create and execute great ideas. Power to lead people of God as God views them and power to explore great resources of Africa for the Africans and beyond. Power of leadership comes from God and discovery of your worth as you study. For wherever the carcass is, there the eagles will be gathered together.[ccxlvii] Do all your struggles now and aim high to live without struggle after. Studentship is not an easy task but the comfort comes after the process.

Sam Adeyemi, a revolutionist for right and godly leadership, writes and I quote, "The development of leadership qualities is a priority in life. When I talk of developing your leadership ability, I think we need to focus on those two dimensions: character and competence. Character is who you are, while competence is your ability to do what you do" He says further, "When leaders have integrity, there is no pretense in public." [ccxlviii] Integrity is not part of school curriculum. Only God can make a man right, yet you have input therein. Why do we have senates who got involved in sexual scandals? Why do we read on newspapers the acts of corruption of people of ethics? Nigeria has leaders who cannot speak the truth because they want to maintain their political office. I used to hear that 'we are the leaders of tomorrow.' Leaders are made from previous leaders. Who will make us the leaders of tomorrow? Are these corrupt souls that have sold their eternity to mammon and devil? If you are godless and ruthless as a student, you are a devotee to wrong leadership already. Money, women, fame, power, and popularity have great grip on any man to misbehave and lose integrity anytime. I would like to quote the word of Gbile Akanni on the nobility of leadership. He says, "The blessing of a nation or a people is tied to the quality of leaders she has. A leader must be a free man. A man who is a prisoner of his conscience cannot stand up to defend righteousness among the people he is leading"[ccxlix] Integrity of the leaders is their credential that must not fail out.

Leaders who uphold integrity will attract critics. Critics are enemies of progress. In your class, home, campus, street, community, we have people who will not live right and always read to stop whoever is doing the right things. Have you ever seen a monument erected to a critic? No! When the critic throws stones, the visionary leaders should take them and build a wall as Nehemiah did in the Bible. [ccl] Great ideas and leaders have a common enemy–the critic. Praise and criticism come and go. Pleasing God is all that matters.[ccli] Do not compromise your right way of life. Continue to preach it; live it to reality. One day, you will become hero of integrity because everyone will have no choice but to accept your ideology of right living.

Innovation distinguishes between a leader and a follower – Steve Jobs

Integrity of the leaders needs refueling – the fear of God. Bible gives clear picture of leaders who have lost fear of God to commit errors. Who are they? They have eyes full of adultery and that cannot cease from sin, enticing unstable souls. They have a heart trained in covetous practices, and are accursed children. They have forsaken the right way and gone astray, following the way of Balaam the son of Beor, who loved the wages of unrighteousness; but he was rebuked for his iniquity: a dumb donkey speaking with a man's voice restrained the madness of the prophet. These are wells without water; clouds carried by a tempest, for whom is reserved the blackness of darkness forever. For when they speak great swelling words of emptiness, they allure through the lusts of the flesh, through lewdness, the ones who have actually escaped from those who live in error.[cclii] The fear of the LORD is the beginning of knowledge, but fools despise wisdom and instruction.[ccliii] As students who are warming up for the leadership seats, let the fear of God rule your mind now in your class duties, campus activities, examination process, etc. God will never use or appoint anyone that is available but not prepared. Be prepared.

Leadership is championship. Soldiers go, soldiers come, and barrack remains the same. Only the relevant leaders will sit for long. Sitting for long does not mean having buttock stock to the chair. It means your great work will speak for you when you retire and expire. Have you ever thought of championing a discovery that will solve African problem? Great leaders are not forgotten; for their works keep their names alive. As you study, keep your vision alive and be a pioneer of new things. A pioneer is a leader.

The leaders that Nigerian needs are ones that will not glue their buttock on seat of power. Africa had produced life presidents and no one dare to challenge them. In Nigeria, we have Gen. Sanni Abacha (on the throne for 5 years until his death);[ccliv] Libya, Col.

Muammar Gadhafi (ruled for 40 years),[cclv] Robert Mugabe of Zimbabwe (first prime minister, 1980-1987, and president from 1987 till date),[cclvi] and others. They see no intelligence or confidence in any other persons than themselves. They refuse to breed other generations for the seat while some make it a family dynasty. A revolution of students with mind of godly leadership will emerge soonest. Can God count on you?

A key ingredient in innovation is the ability to challenge authority and break rules of idleness and mediocrity with contentment with status quo – Vivck Wadlwa

Nigeria needs high level resulted-oriented leaders, not propagandists. Leadership is not only on the majestic seat at Aso Rock Villa, Abuja. Of course, no! We have leaders in different sectors of the nation that are silent-changers. Their result is calling attention of people to them. You can be a successful leader in your career. Dangote[cclvii] is ruling Nigeria economy because he is daily producing consumable goods for consumers–you and I. When knowledge is converted to commercialized innovation, leadership roles will emerge. Start to think of what you can produce to rule any sector in Nigeria. I felt bad whenever I remember the rigorous work with little pay and harsh treatment that the Nigerian casual workers received from foreigners that still come and enslave us in our land. Especially the Lebanese, they are harsh, inhuman, and money-driven, yet Nigerians have no choice but to remain loyal under a life-threatening working condition. Augustine Etafo, the National President of Construction and Civil Engineering Senior Staff, expressed concern over inhuman treatment of Nigerian workers by multinational on casualization while their foreign counterparts smile home with all the benefits accrued to the same job Nigerians do.[cclviii] "Suffering and smiling" syndrome will continue until and unless you, my reader, take this challenge to face your studies, discover and develop ideas that will end this dehumanization called casual labour. Nigerians count on you.

EXPECTED PRODUCTS THREE –
CONTEXTUALIZATION OF TECHNOLOGY TO AFRICA

Africa is unique in her understanding and consumption. We celebrate what we know and refuse to add more. If the students on Africa shore discover great facts and discoveries, our people do not quickly accept home-made products because it does have foreign-bit. Truly, there is standard-based product from other countries like US, UK, Dubai, etc. These countries do not compromise standard for anything. In the world market, Africa, especially Nigeria is seen as dumping ground for inferior and sub-standard products because we are foreign-crazy. We import almost everything we use in the country, even the toothpick is on the import list. Now that the Nigeria currency is falling in value to dollar, it is expected of everyone to develop home-made products to boost our economy both within and outside our shore. I know especially that Nigeria is blessed with thinking-tanks that can invent, produce, design and create new products that will beat the world standard. It starts from you and I as we commit our might to invention. Do you have an idea? If yes, what step have you taken to materialize the idea? Is the idea foreign even within you? I mean you do not even see Nigeria as the beneficiaries of the products.

When you think of any products that can affect the economy, you must think altogether the standard of the product. Though, people may not patronize at first, but as time flies, they will see the value as equal to other countries'. Contextualization of technology to Africa is needed to boost our economy. In Nigeria, we have brains that can imitate any products. If you go to Onitsha and Aba market in the eastern part of Nigeria, you will appreciate technology. There are great inventors and imitators in the land but no fund to standardize the production. All that they produce are still foreign made. The technology idea is not totally ours. Most of the tricks are hidden from us because they will never sell the idea to Africa at once. We are still technologically enslaved by US, China, Malaysia, India, Dubai, etc. These countries will employ our citizens to couple what they produced.

The main idea is behind the veil. We need Nigerians that will research and develop new ways of doing all these things without these counties. Malaysia did it. And today, they are out of developing countries of the world. The country is skyrocketing in industrialization and technology today. Nigeria can be better.

During a career talk in my school, one of my students boldly affirmed that "Nigeria's main problem is production and nothing more. We have raw material left idle for exporting and consumption alone."[cclix] We need service of mechatronics, mechanical, system and civil engineers to design and build machines that will convert raw materials to finished products according to the world standard. Then we have Nigeria-made product available. What is the state of your mind on Nigeria-made product? Use Nigeria-made. Produce Nigeria-made. As a student who thinks to change things, you must patronize this product to know the strength, weakness, opportunity and threats in the world market. Think the best as your use them.

Our leaders travel abroad for health care while the citizens die daily on inadequate and bad health gadgets and equipment within the country. An accused or prosecuted politicians that had case in court would still plead to travel abroad for health care. Why not in Nigeria? They know that their lives are not safe here. I know, nemesis will catch up with them on day. Nigerian health sector is living on old machines and equipment that is why health workers go on labour strike.[cclx] Truly, we do not have current machines that can handle health maintenance in Nigeria and Africa. We depend on India, UK, US and other developed nations for our health care machines. What a shame! I read a pathetic story of how a promising Nigeria lady died in India for surgery. If all these machines are invented, innovated and produced in Nigeria, this lady will be alive. From the Punch Newspaper with this headline, "Our daughter's journey of no return to India – Parents of 26-year-old ago died during surgery in Indian hospital".[cclxi] Miss Chineye Nwafor, who had big dreams of becoming an accomplished author, just graduated from the University of Abuja with degree on English Language and about to go for NYSC, went to Indian hospital for leg surgery to correct her left limb which was severely shortened after an accident about ten years ago. The accident broke her femur and she had a surgery which involved the insertion of k-nail (iron) to support the bone. The inserted iron broke and she needed another surgery to remove the broken iron and correct the limb that had caused her a lot of pains for years. So in August 19th, 2015, she arrived Indian for the surgery but the family had difficulty in making money transfer to the hospital of about $6,000/N1.9m, which were later paid before they started the surgery after much pain in 28th September, 2015 and she was operated the next day. In high spirit, the family waited for her arrival but Nwafor could not. However, on October 9, 2015, their hopes and dreams were rudely cut short. Nwafor was pronounced dead ten days after the surgery in Fortis Hospital, New Delhi. She had difficulty with the insertion and returned to the hospital for attention and later the doctors declared that she was breathless and the mother was told. She (the mother) said, "I felt the world had come to an end, even in my state of shock, the best the hospital could do was to demand for an additional payment from me as cost of trying to revive Chineye. When I walked into the room where she laid, I discovered they had removed the oxygen and stuffed near nostrils with cotton wool while her body was still very warm. I tried and begged them to try and administer more medical care to resuscitate her but they told me that there was nothing they could do." Chineye died. She could not live to publish her novels, marry her fiancé and give birth to her future great kids. Many more lives die daily on foreign soils for health care and no one cares. I care, that is why I write this book. Why are you schooling? School because there is a problem to solve. We need technological innovation for medical gadgets. Fill your mind with the passion to save the unborn child of Africa.

Sourcing for materials is another area that African students need to look into. Do we have raw materials for our invention? If yes, do we have them in abundance? Can we test run to build invention on them? There is need to explore our environment for our raw materials. We have iron ore, gold, coal, zinc, etc. in Nigeria and environs. We just need to design, construct and build machines for our products. You can start to think in this direction. We have a lot of waste products in Africa because we are wasteful in nature. I want to believe we are t wasteful. Why the contradiction? It is because we do not know what the waste can become. Every material is a potential product and every waste is also a potential product if recycled properly. Even our daily urine can be recycled through biotechnology. This will lead to the next expected product from students with optimistic mind for African development.

EXPECTED PRODUCTS FOUR – RESEARCH AND DEVELOPMENT

Research and Development (R&D) is a process undertaken by an organization before the launch of a product; goods, idea and service. Research is usually scientific.[cclxii] Research starts from the mind. When a topic is given in the class, genius will immediately begin to search for likely solution of what, where, when and how. The solution of any problems begins with you passion to do something. The readiness to go out and source for what comes to mind is the basic foundation for research work. What you conceive is what you will develop. No research no development. It is pity that most of our tertiary institutions only develop another persons' research. It is good to build on precedence. Nevertheless, we need to re-discover what had been discovered from ages. There is need to contextualize the aging discovery to our days and context.

Africa needs students who are original in approach to research. Let's start with academic work. Do you see any reason to originally source for your data? Do you love travelling to the place of primary source of the research? Do you enjoy deep thinking over your research work than 'copy and paste' approach of some students? Do you plagiarize? My good reader, I am a party to clean and sound academic paper work that you will be able to stand tall to defend. And I want you to keep your stand with me on the matter.

If you will begin to think research and development, maybe you can get solution for Nigeria. Let me share some facts and figures with as at 2009 from Microsoft Encarta. Nigeria lived on agriculture many years ago like king among many countries of Africa. Farm workers in northern Nigeria harvest peanuts. Nigeria's economy was largely based upon agriculture before oil revenues transformed the economy during the 1960s and 1970s. Today, Nigeria must import food to meet the needs of its people. Another part of Nigeria, Cross River has vast areas and they were cleared for agricultural use, and timber harvesters cut down many valuable hardwood trees. At one time, the forest supported a huge wildlife population, including elephants, wild boar, buffalo, and leopards. As a result of deforestation and habitat loss, Nigeria ranks second in the world in the number of mammal species threatened with extinction. Despite its positive trade balance, the Nigerian economy is burdened with massive external debt amounting in 2002 to $31.6 billion, most of it owed to other governments and multilateral agencies. The government has had difficulty meeting its yearly debt payments. Nigeria's yearly debt-servicing bill, including arrears and interest, can rival the country's total export earnings. Most of the debt stems from extravagant government megaprojects prior to the mid-1980s and from imports of consumer goods. The sudden collapse of oil prices in the early 1980s made Nigerian financial matters worse. In recent years international lenders have forced Nigeria to introduce reforms to restructure its economy. Infant mortality rate is 94 deaths per 1,000 live births (2008 estimate). Population per physician was 3,715 people as at 2004; population per hospital bed was 599 people as at 1990; literacy rate total 70.7 percent (2005 estimate). [cclxiii] Nigerian fight and protest for development, but Ben Okiri, a Nigerian novelist, short-story writer, and poet, says, "A man's greatest battles are the ones he fights within himself."[cclxiv] And I believe this - Within the mind is the real battle ground. If you win from within, the battle is over. He further adds from his book, *The Famished Road,* that, "The only power poor people have is their hunger."[cclxv] It might be factual to some Nigerians but to you and me, it is just a provoking statement that will throw us into profound thinking that will eventually to stop hunger rather than being slaves to propagandists in caftan.

Research and development is the solution to African poverty. Have you ever asked why your community is enduring bad environmental degradation? Why do Nigerians have 46% life expectancy? It is because you and I had stopped to think proactively. Instead, we daily abuse government; criticize the politicians, protesting against fuel price hiking, bad hospital infrastructures, etc. What have you thought within you as solution to save the next generation from what your fathers' generation did not do? You are a victim of their negligence and complacency with old boom. Nigeria did not plan to research to what other things can hold on her economy. There was no foresight of crude oil price fall. In fact, the fall has affected all sectors in the country. You can stop this evil how? Get the basic education. Daily set a dream target in your mind. Do not be distracted with what is happening. Be proactive to materialize your dream to idea and idea to product. Convert you academic excellence to commercialized innovations that will set Nigeria and Africa free. Do not ignore any research opportunity. Be curious and experimental. Ask questions on anything that you do not understand; it is never a crime. Keep record of your discoveries and gradually develop them. How? Seek knowledge from the expert through seminars, workshop, instructional video, books, online pages, or if there is need to travel to the source for more explanation. Be driven by your dream – to solve problems and not to ignore or add to them. Africa is still very fertile for research and development.

CHAPTER THIRTEEN
GOD AND STUDENT'S MIND

I heard a story many years ago about a man who was driving his truck on a narrow mountain road. To his right was a cliff that dropped hurriedly nearly 500 feet to a valley below. As the driver rounded a curve, he suddenly lost control of the vehicle. It jumped over the side and bounced down the mountain, bursting into flames at the bottom. Although the terrified man was ejected as his truck went over the edge, he managed to grab a bush that grew near the top. There he was, desperately holding the small limb and dangling dangerously over the hole. After trying to pull himself up for several minutes, he called out in desperation, *"Is anybody there?"* In a few seconds, the thundering voice of the Lord echoed across the mountain. "Yes, I am here," He said. "What do you want?" The man pleaded, "Please save me! I can't hold on much longer!" After another agonizing pause, the voice said, "All right. I will save you. But first you must turn loose of the limb and trust Me to catch you. Just release your grip now. My hands will be under you." The dangling man looked over his shoulder at the burning truck in the valley below, and then he called out, "Is anybody else there?"[cclxvi] Have you ever weighed God's reply and then wanted to ask, "Is anybody else there?" We think we know what we need in every moment, but God often has other ideas.

Western civilization is for the first time in its history in danger of dying. The reason is spiritual. It is losing its life, its soul; that soul was the Christian faith….We do apologetics not to save the church but to save the world – Peter Kreeft and Ron Tacelli

Ideas were born by God. God is before idea and shall be when all ideas will be of no use. He conceived the world without the counsel of any man. He structurally created the earth from scratch to finish without stress. He was not short of materials, labour or power. He is a good planner and executor. God knows first thing as first. God made the universe out of big idea of making a best place for man. He made provision before creation of man. The creation was in sequential flow. He made man like Himself. There is no imperfect in man. David said, "For You (God) formed my inward parts; You covered me in my mother's womb. I will praise You, for I am fearfully and wonderfully made; marvelous are Your works, and that my soul knows very well. My frame was not hidden from You, when I was made in secret, and skillfully wrought in the lowest parts of the earth. Your eyes saw my substance, being yet unformed. And in Your book they all were written, the days fashioned for me, when as yet there were none of them. How precious also are Your thoughts to me, O God! How great is the sum of them![cclxvii] Whenever I looked at myself and the beauty of mankind, I salute God's creativity.

God made man's head with bones that can strongly protect the brain. Brain is just an ordinary flesh that is sensitive to any shock, and then God put shock absorber in the head. Brain has sensitive work yet the neurosurgeons cannot physically see the work—mind, thought, behaviour and emotions. All human emotions—including love, hate, fear, anger, elation, and sadness—are controlled by the brain. I have not seen brain surgeons who will be able to remove behaviour from the brain or cut off bad emotions from man such as hate, envy, fear, anger, etc. If they can do such surgery, then our world would have become a better place for right minded people. Also, I wish they should be able to detect a man's thought in the brain and reprogramme the mind with another thought. One time, I was brainstorming and asked myself a question, "Why do people think and plan evil against one another and also execute the evil without anyone's knowledge?" Then I thought of an invention—a device that will be transplanted inside the body of man, connected to the brain where the mind is. The device will have an external speaker that will be at body rear. This speaker will be disconnected from the earing organ of the host—which means as he thinks, the external speaker will voice out the thought and the next person beside him will hear clearly. God is God. He never committed the creation of man to man. If He did, man would have misuse the opportunity. He gave everyone equal opportunities—24 hours, brain with sound mind, body to move around and creativity to make our world better.

If God owns all things—including you, then mind of students should take a cue from Him for strength. Why? God sees without barrier. He created the raw materials you are thinking of making something from. He had foresight of your thought before you even think it. Psalmist confirms the intelligence of God, "O LORD, You have searched me and known me. You know my sitting down and my rising up; You understand my thought afar off. You comprehend my path and my lying down, and are acquainted with all my ways. For there is not a word on my tongue, but behold, O LORD, You know it altogether."[cclxviii] God is supernatural—beyond human rationale. Every student that desires dream fulfillment must connect to God for strength.

In the Bible also, we have great heroes who leaned on God for wisdom. Wisdom is the creativity of the mind. Noah was called to build an ark. There was no pre-introduction of his career that he studied carpentry and building technology. Yet God commissioned him to build an ark that would contain all animals and men for days. What God needs from student is obedient and willing heart. Noah did not argue with God because with God all things are possible.

Solomon was a young boy and inexperienced to rule a nation. He prayed to God for His help, "Now, O LORD my God, You have made Your servant king instead of my father David, but I am a little child; I do not know how to go out or come in. And Your servant is in the midst of Your people whom You have chosen, a great people, too numerous to be numbered or counted. Therefore give to Your servant an understanding heart to judge Your people that I may discern between good and evil. For who is able to judge this great people of Yours?"[cclxix] God answered his prayers. He became the wisest king in history of Israel. He built temple of Jerusalem. He wrote books, proverbs and poems. He artistically designed the temple and palace with costly stones. He engaged brained ones in his kingdom.

Another hero that connected to God for strength is Gideon. Gideon was a blunt and fearful coward. He did not know he could do what he did after. He allowed God to help him in fulfilling his life purpose. Gideon led few army—300 soldiers—to fight great nations. He lost confidence in human reasoning. How? What God commanded him to do was unreasonable; going to battle with pot, trumpet and torchlight. Confidently I say this, God knows the best way to the stardom. Only the students who queue behind God will see clearly the right path to their dreams. Gideon won all his battles without a fight.

We live in what may be the most anti-intellectual period in the history of Western civilization.... We must have passion–indeed hearts on fire for the things of God. But that passion must resist with intensity the anti-intellectual spirit of the world – R. C. Sproul

If you have admitted that God has influence and control over mind, dream and the future of students, I have these pieces of advice for you.

Love God

Let your move into discovery and invention start with God and end with Him. Why? Those inventors who relied solely on what God could do through them had changed the world since. They lived to glorify God in their works. Only a fool will say there is no God. Let your love for God be seen; do not place Him on shadow. Remember He says and knows your thought before it comes alive.

We are having a revival of feelings but not of the knowledge of God. The church today is more guided by feelings than by convictions. We value enthusiasm more than informed commitment – 1980 Gallup Poll on Religion

Love God's creature

If you confess you love God without loving His creature, you are just cunningly outsmarting God. And no one can be smarter than

God. Your love can only be seen on the face of men. What are you planning to setup, produce, formulate, write or invent? Is it to pollute moral, spiritual or physical life of men? Our musicians and celebrities have forgotten that the knowledge, skill and sonorous voices are embedded in them to save human race for God; not against God. Today, inventors are producing lethal weapons that can annihilate human race within seconds. They discover tactics to overrule nations with terrorism. The homosexuals are formulating policies to stop human race reproduction through gay sex. Why are you studying what you chose as career? If you love God and man, you will graduate and be compassionate in your approach to fellow man. Some doctors and nurses are heartless in their profession. If they love God, human life will be precious in their hands. Civil engineers, who had privilege to construct roads, did substandard work to keep the monetary change in their bank accounts but they were not moved how lives get lost on the road every day. Politicians, who are voted to save lives, ignore masses to hunger. Where is their love for God? Yet they are members of either a church or mosque, having form of godliness by devil underneath. Nigerians are dying because students are studying to be great without God in their minds. You cannot change the world that you did create. How? You first need to know the Creator as your Lord and Saviour and have the passion of a new Nigeria in your mind before you can be gracious to save any creatures. The mind of student with love of God and man will become zealous and progressive to fulfilling eternal agenda of human salvation through our Lord Jesus Christ.

Love His word

Bible is the written word of God to all men. As a student who dreams great about tomorrow, there are tendency of abnormalities on the process to the top, only the word of God you know will keep you obedient to God, truthful to the cause of your dream, loyal to your boss, devoted to your values of uprightness, committed to innovation that saves lives and patriotic to the nation. God's word has no alternative when life's challenges surface. You need this word as encouragement, power and confidence as you're journeying to the top.

The God of the Jew was to exist in the Word and through the Word, an unprecedented conception requiring the highest order of abstract thinking – Neil Postman

Be done with self-reliance

Wisdom is the key word in the mind of students and inventors. Wisdom cannot be adulterated. Only God gives. If any of you lacks wisdom, let him ask of God, who gives to all liberally and without reproach, and it will be given to him.[cclxx] Wisdom had been with God and still with God. Solomon did not rely on riches, self-discovered wisdom and family fame; he called on God for divine wisdom and he had Him. Who is wisdom? Is it a thing or a being? Solomon in the book of Proverbs divinely realized who wisdom was. Wisdom himself spoke with Solomon, "I, wisdom, dwell with prudence, and find out knowledge and discretion. The fear of the LORD is to hate evil; pride and arrogance and the evil way and the perverse mouth I hate. Counsel is mine, and sound wisdom; I am understanding, I have strength. By me, kings reign and rulers decree justice. By me, princes rule, and nobles, all the judges of the earth. I love those who love me, and those who seek me diligently will find me. Riches and honor are with me, enduring riches and righteousness. My fruit is better than gold, yes, than fine gold, and my revenue than choice silver. I traverse the way of righteousness, In the midst of the paths of justice, that I may cause those who love me to inherit wealth, that I may fill their treasuries. "The LORD possessed me at the beginning of His way, before His works of old. I have been established from everlasting, from the beginning, before there was ever an earth. When there were no depths I was brought forth, when there were no fountains abounding with water. Before the mountains were settled, Before the hills, I was brought forth; while as yet He had not made the earth or the fields, or the primeval dust of the world. When He prepared the heavens, I was there, when He drew a circle on the face of the deep, when He established the clouds above, when He strengthened the fountains of the deep, when He assigned to the sea its limit, so that the waters would not transgress His command, When He marked out the foundations of the earth, then I was beside Him as a master craftsman; and I was daily His delight, rejoicing always before Him, rejoicing in His inhabited world, And my delight was with the sons of men. "Now therefore, listen to me, my children, For blessed are those who keep my ways. Hear instruction and be wise, and do not disdain it. Blessed is the man who listens to me, watching daily at my gates, waiting at the posts of my doors. For whoever finds me finds life, And obtains favor from the LORD; but he who sins against me wrongs his own soul; all those who hate me love death."[cclxxi] Do you desire this wisdom? Wisdom is Jesus Christ. If you have Him as your Lord, He will come to you and fill your mind with wisdom to solve problems that you are created for. As a student, take this advice from me – "Trust in the LORD with all your heart, and lean not on your own understanding; in all your ways acknowledge Him, And He shall direct your paths. Do not be wise in your own eyes; Fear the LORD and depart from evil. It will be health to your flesh, and strength to your bones."[cclxxii]

Unreasonable and absurd ways of life... are truly an offense to God – William Law

Stand with God

In this hour when things of God are not well spoken again while we promote secularism, God needs you by His side. J. P. Moreland, [cclxxiii] an evangelist who apologetically standing against secularism wrote in his lecture notes that what Government of the day says that, "If your religious beliefs work for you, that's great, but don't impose them on others." However, Moreland argues that, no one would say that a scientist is imposing anything on anyone when he says that water is H20 or that 2+2=4. Nor would these claims be viewed as private opinions whose sole value was their usefulness for those who believe them. Why? Because only science supposedly deals with facts, truth, and reason, but religion and ethics allegedly deal with private, subjective opinions. We must rededicate ourselves to being deeply spiritual people of whom it can truly be said that "Christ is formed in you".[cclxxiv] If we are going to be wise, spiritual students need to prepare to meet the crises of our age; we must be studying students of God's word, learning and building Christian community that values the life of the mind of students. We need to stand for God even in this collapsing global system of civilizations. As man of secularity tries to pull down divinity, you must stand with and for God. John the Baptist refused to keep quiet when evil was the order of the day. He said, "He (God) must increase, but I must decrease."[cclxxv]

LAST WORD

Nigeria is still very young and expectant. The African nations are waiting for investors, discoverers, initiators, innovators and researchers that will give the expected products with standard. Poverty is not part of our community; it is human creation. We should go to school, study hard and brainstorm way-out to produce commercialized innovation. Do not follow bad friends who have no passionate dream like yours. Flock with like-minded students in the school and community. Pray and believe God. The world at large is at the waiting room for you at the stardom.

CONNECT TO GOD
LEAVE THE FAT ANTELOPE BEHIND

A warrior was hunting antelope, and he shot a large buck. But when he brought the animal back to the shore of the Congo, his canoe was gone. Without a boat, he couldn't cross the river, so he waited for help. Soon a fisherman came by in a small boat. He was willing to carry the man to the other side, but the antelope would be too big for his boat. "Then I will wait," said the hunter. No other rescuer came along, so the hunter decided to camp out until morning. He cut a piece from the dead antelope for his dinner. But before he could eat it, a lion came and killed him. What a great lost! Are you amazed at the foolish decision of this warrior who lost his dear life to greediness of keeping an antelope? In fact, he did not value his life at all.

The antelope in this story stands for sin in your life. It is a very big time and opportunity to enjoy lust and fun of sin. Sin is very sweet and charming. It has power to keep its prey from seeing well. It tastes pleasant but deep down it becomes soar and bitter. Sin has power to reform itself so that its prey will not be free. In today's world, a lot of antelope opportunities have camouflaged themselves as civilization and modernization but their mission is destruction. For example, sin of sexual immorality is available on the street, in the campus, on phone, entertainment world and even in the worship centers. Smoking of cigarettes is bad and harmful yet it is advertised and promoted. Alcoholism causes a lot of disorderliness in the society yet it is advertised and promoted through sponsoring of youthful programmes. A free drink with toll-free partying is a big antelope of sin that will hinder your journey in this life and life after. Sin comes so cheat but its indebtedness enslaves. Fashion and trend come to turn your heart against your life purpose. Since you have been enslaved by the trend, have you be satisfied? All these are antelopes that hold down a mighty warrior like you at the sea of life. God created you to impact this world but your sin is too heavy to cross the river with you.

Dear friend, it is better to drop the unnecessary affection for sin and pleasure at the shore and cross over alive to fulfillment because the opportunity of getting a boat may never repeat itself. What is your life? Hear what the scripture says, "How foolish it is to say, Today or tomorrow we will go into this town, and be there for a year and do business there and get wealth: when you are not certain what will take place tomorrow. What is your life? It is a mist, which is seen for a little time and then is gone" (James 4:13-14). You may still want to say I have some years to spend. When I get old I will leave sins aside and serve God. Hear what the preacher says, "Remember now thy Creator in the days of thy youth, while the evil days come not, nor the years draw nigh, when thou shalt say, I have no pleasure in them" (Eccl. 12:1). Time waits for no one. The fisher man with his boat may not wait for long. "For everything there is a fixed time, and a time for everything under the sun. A time for birth and a time for death; a time for planting and a time for uprooting; a time to put to death and a time to make well; a time for pulling down and a time for building up" (Eccl. 3:1-3).The only escape boat from sinful life is to believe and accept Jesus Christ as your Saviour and Lord. He has power to save you from the yoke of sin. Do not sleep over this matter as the warrior did lose his life and do not sit to eat the antelope because the lion, "...your great accuser, the Devil, is going about like a roaring lion to see whom he can devour" (1 Peter 3:8).

If you are ready, just wholeheartedly say this prayer: Lord, Jesus Christ, I know I am a sinner that you died for. I was lost in sin because I was under the control of the evil one and ignorance. Now I know the truth and I want to make heaven, kindly accept me and cleanse my sins away. Give me access into your Book of Life and guide me till I die or You come. I confess therefore that you are my Saviour and Lord. Thank you for saving me. Amen.

Now that you are saved from the sins and penalty of sinful life, daily love the Lord Jesus with your heart and know more about Him till He comes. Shun bad ones and find new friends in your new faith in Christ.

ABOUT THE AUTHOR

Allen Olatunde is presently a chaplain in Patterson Memorial Baptist Grammar School, Idi-Aba, Abeokuta, Ogun State. He was once an associate Pastor of Zion Baptist Church, Minna, Niger State and Chaplain and tutor of her school. He had served in the Teenagers' Ministry of two churches. He was an award winner of NYSC State Honour Award 2006 at Cross River State. He graduated from The Nigerian Baptist Theological Seminary, Ogbomoso with Master of Divinity in Missiology. He is an alumnus of The Polytechnic Ibadan, Oyo State with HND in Business Administration and Management Studies.

Allen Olatunde is a certified Peer Education Trainer by UNICEF and also an ICT compliant. He is a teacher of God's Word, who is deeply committed to discipleship, cross cultural missions, social ministry and church media. He labours also in Africa! GLOW Missions Connect, a ministry to the obscure world. He is a seasoned writer. He has authored two books; When I Seek God's Face and Career Choice Made Easy for Secondary School Students. He is passionate about creativity and innovation among teens. He had organized seminars and workshops for young adults and students on how to discover skills tagged "Creative Awake." He promotes excellence in technological innovation through annual award presentation.

He is happily married to Temitayo, and together with their children, Emmanuel and Jemimah, live in Abeokuta, Nigeria.

i Microsoft Encarta Dictionary 2009. Microsoft Corporation, 1993-2008.

ii Vincent Norman Peale. You Can If You Think You Can. UK: The Random House Group Limited, 1974.

iii John Perry. "Philosophy of Mind." Microsoft Encarta 2009 [DVD]. Redmond, WA: Microsoft Corporation, 2008.

iv Psalm 139:14

v Toga W. Arthur. Microsoft Encarta 2009. 1993-2008 Microsoft Corporation

vi Walter Mischel. Niven Professor of Humane Letters in Psychology at Columbia University. Research interests include personality and self-regulation. World renowned for marshmellow experiment in the area of delayed gratification. Served as president of the Association for Psychological Science (2007-08) and as editor of the Psychological Review (2000-03). Recipient of National Institute of Mental Health Merit Award (1989 up to 2009; awarded twice, sequentially) and the University of Louisville Grawemeyer Award for Psychology (2011). Publications include Introduction to Personality: Toward an Integration (2004).

vii Walter Mischel. "Psychology - Encyclopædia Britannica." Encyclopædia Britannica Ultimate Reference Suite. Chicago: Encyclopædia Britannica, 2014.

viii Professor of Philosophy, University of Maryland, College Park. Author of Contemporary Philosophy of Mind: A Contentiously Classical Approach and others.

ix Georges Rey "mind, philosophy of." Encyclopædia Britannica. Encyclopædia Britannica Ultimate Reference Suite. Chicago: Encyclopædia Britannica, 2014.

x Sixth sense is an intangible sensory tool which serves as our internal navigator, knows and reveals the path for enabling and allowing our heartfelt desires to take tangible and measurable form, yet often becomes silenced by enabling the 5 physical senses to dictate and determine in our minds what is real and true in life – Super Conscious Mind. www.abundance-and-happiness.com/the-sixth-sense.html Cited 6th July, 2016 by 5.00pm.

xi Genius in psychology is a person of extraordinary intellectual power and has definitions in terms of intelligence quotient (IQ) which are based on research originating in the early 1900s. In 1916 the American psychologist Lewis M. Terman set the IQ for "potential genius" at 140 and above, a level exhibited by about 1 in every 250 people. Leta Hollingworth, an American psychologist who studied the nature and nurture of genius, proposed an IQ of 180 as the threshold—a level that, at least theoretically, is exhibited by only about one in every two million people.

xii Wright Brothers were American brothers, inventors, and aviation pioneers who achieved the first powered, sustained, and controlled airplane flight (1903). Wilbur Wright (April 16, 1867, near Millville, Indiana, U.S.—May 30, 1912, Dayton, Ohio) and his brother Orville Wright (August 19, 1871, Dayton—January 30, 1948, Dayton) also built and flew the first fully practical airplane, 1905.

xiii Tom D. Crouch. "Wright brothers - Encyclopædia Britannica." Encyclopædia Britannica Ultimate Reference Suite. Chicago: Encyclopædia Britannica, 2014.

xiv Vincent Norman Peale. You Can If You Think You Can. UK: The Random House Group Limited, 1974.

xv Sam Adeyemi. Ideas Rules The World. Lagos: Pneuma Publishing Ltd, 2000.

xvi Some of the learning ways were taught during Godly Brain Hour at Shalom Baptist Church, Ilorin in November, 2014.

xvii My experience with co-corps member at Cross River in 2006 who studied Computer Physic and could not operate computer successfully

xviii Microsoft Encarta Encyclopedia 2009. Microsoft Corporation, 1993-2008.

xix Sam Adeyemi. Multiply Your Success Lead. Lagos: Pneuma Publishing Ltd, 2009.

xx I learnt this when I was in secondary school and close observation of the animal

xxi Brian Tracy. Eat That Frog. Benin City: Joint Heirs Publications, 2007.

xxii Punch Newspaper. A student with First class in university at Ekiti State.

xxiii Sam Adeyemi. Multiply Your Success Lead. Lagos: Pneuma Publishing Ltd, 2009.

xxiv Philippians 4:13

xxv Brian Tracy. Eat That Frog. Benin City: Joint Heirs Publications, 2007.

xxvi Brian Tracy. Eat That Frog. Benin City: Joint Heirs Publications, 2007.

xxvii Mike Murdock. The Assignment. Oklahoma: Albury Publishing, 1997.

xxviii Microsoft Encarta Dictionary. Microsoft Corporation, 1993-2008.

xxix Brian Tracy. Eat That Frog. Benin City: Joint Heirs Publications, 2007.

xxx Joshua 1:6-7

xxxi Philippians 3:13-14

xxxii Vincent Norman Peale. You Can If You Think You Can. UK: The Random House Group Limited, 1974.

xxxiii Vincent Norman Peale. You Can If You Think You Can. UK: The Random House Group Limited, 1974.

xxxiv Isaiah 6:6

xxxv Microsoft Encarta Dictionary 2009. Microsoft Corporation, 1993-2008.

xxxvi Brian Tracy. Eat That Frog. Benin City: Joint Heirs Publications, 2007.

xxxvii Sam Adeyemi. Multiply Your Success Lead. Lagos: Pneuma Publishing Ltd, 2009.

xxxviii Allen Olatunde. Career Choice Made Easy. Abeokuta: Africa! GLOW Missions Connect, 2015.

xxxix When I was in The Polytechnic Ibadan, Personnel Course Lecturer, 2004

xl Vincent Norman Peale. You Can If You Think You Can. UK: The Random House Group Limited, 1974.

xli It happened at Osun State Polytechnic, Iree, Osun State, 2000.

xlii I was moved to start a crusade of young ones who will dream cure for Ebola that killed thousands in west Africa and Nigeria in 2014-2015

xliii Microsoft Encarta 2009. Microsoft Corporation, 1993-2008.

xliv Microsoft Encarta 2009. Microsoft Corporation, 1993-2008.

xlv Microsoft Encarta 2009. Microsoft Corporation, 1993-2008.

xlvi My decision when I was at NYSC Orientation Camp at Obubra, Cross Rivers State in February, 2006.
xlvii Proverbs 19:24
xlviii Matthew 26:41
xlix Song of Solomon 2:7
l Allen Olatunde. A Paper to the Parent on Child and Freedom. Patterson Memorial Baptist Grammar School, Abeokuta, 2015
li Fiction story formed to clarify the point
lii It happened at one secondary school at Ibadan around 2005
liii When I was in secondary at Loyola College Ibadan, 1996
liv Microsoft Encarta Dictionary 2009. Microsoft Corporation, 1993-2008.
lv Sam Adeyemi. Multiply Your Success Lead. Lagos: Pneuma Publishing Ltd, 2009.
lvi Sam Adeyemi. Multiply Your Success Lead. Lagos: Pneuma Publishing Ltd, 2009.
lvii Michael Catt. Courageous Living: Dare to Take a Stand. Nashville: B & H Publishing Group, 2011.
lviii Allen Olatunde. Career Choice Made Easy. Abeokuta: Africa! GLOW Missions Connect, 2015.
lix At Latter Time Campus Fellowship at Iree, Osun State, 2001.
lx At Nigerian Baptist Theological Seminary, Ogbomoso, 2009-2012
lxi Microsoft Encarta Dictionary 2009. Microsoft Corporation, 1993-2008.
lxii Sharf, Richard S. "Psychotherapy." Microsoft Encarta 2009 [DVD]. Redmond, WA: Microsoft Corporation, 2008.
lxiii Allen Olatunde. Career Choice Made Easy. Abeokuta: Africa! GLOW Missions Connect, 2015
lxiv Mike and Amarbel Ubi. Why Singles Mingle. Lagos: J.V.C Publication, 2003.
lxv NERDC New Policy 2015 Curriculum
lxvi Praise George. Making It Work: Secrets of Successful Relationships. Lagos: Success World Ltd, 2004.
lxvii Ferdinand Oyono. The Old Man and The Medal. London: Heinemann, 1956.
lxviii Microsoft Encarta 2009.
lxix World Kidney Day at Patterson Memorial Baptist Grammar School, Abeokuta, 2016
lxx On AIT TV around late 2015 seeking for monetary help from the masses
lxxi Proverbs 20:1
lxxii Proverbs 23:21
lxxiii Proverbs 23:19-20; 29-30
lxxiv www.tabac-stop-center.com
lxxv www.healthline.com
lxxvi From Christian programme on 101.9 Rock City FM, Abeokuta, June, 2016
lxxvii My lecturer' advice at personnel management class The Polytechnic Ibadan, 2000
lxxviii www.marcandangel.com Cited 5th July, 2016
lxxix Loyola College Ibadan school 'c' as we used to called the class, 1996.
lxxx Joyce Meyer. Conflict Free Living. US: Charisma House, 2008
lxxxi Bimbo Odukoya. How to Handle Rejection. Lagos: Grace Springs Africa Publishers, 2006.
lxxxii Mike and Amarbel Ubi. Why Singles Mingle. Lagos: J.V.C Publication, 2003.
lxxxiii My mother used to tell me "Remember the son/daughter of whom you are" and it saved me from students' riot in 2001 because I returned back to school when the voice sounded in my ear.
lxxxiv Joyce Meyer. Conflict Free Living. US: Charisma House, 2008
lxxxv Myles Munroe. God's Big Idea. Bahamas: Destiny Image Publishers, 2008.
lxxxvi Myles Munroe. God's Big Idea. Bahamas: Destiny Image Publishers, 2008.
lxxxvii Microsoft Encarta 2009. History Timelines
lxxxviii www.supermemo.com 5th June, 2016 by 4.13pm
lxxxix http://www.geniusawakening.com/genius-brain/genius-brain-vs-normal-brain/ 5th June, 2016 by 4.13pm
xc http://www.geniusawakening.com/genius-brain/genius-brain-vs-normal-brain/ 5th June, 2016 by 4.13pm
xci http://www.geniusawakening.com/genius-brain/genius-brain-vs-normal-brain/ 5th June, 2016 by 4.13pm
xcii http://www.geniusawakening.com/genius-brain/genius-brain-vs-normal-brain/ 5th June, 2016 by 4.13pm
xciii Andreason Nancy. Secrets From The Brains Of 13 Creative Geniuses. http://www.fastcompany.com/3032830/the-future-of- work/secrets-from-the-brains-of-13-creative-geniuses 5th June, 2016 by 4.23pm
xciv www.theatlantic.com/magazine/archive/2014/07/secrets-of-the-creative-brain Cited 5th July, 2016 by 4.45pm
xcv http://www.american.edu/training/ Cited 13th July, 2016 by 4.32pm.
xcvi Microsoft Encarta 2009
xcvii Ken Robinson. Out of Our Minds: Learning to be Creative. Capstone Publishing Ltd (a Wiley company), 2011.
xcviii Robert W. Weisberg. Creativity: Understanding Innovation in Problem Solving, Science, Invention, and the Arts. John Wiley & Sons, 12 Jun 2006.
xcix Psalm 139:14
c Mary Shelley was British novelist, short story writer, dramatist, essayist, biographer, travel writer and editor of poem and philosophy books. www.goodread.com/quotes/tag/invention Cited 20th July, 2016 by 8.40pm
ci https://www.naij.com/58826.html Cited 20th July, 2016 by 8.40pm
cii http://nigerianuniversityscholarships.com/ Cited 20th July, 2016 by 8.43pm
ciii http://nigerianuniversityscholarships.com/ Cited 20th July, 2016 by 8.45pm
civ http://listernaija.com Cited 20th July, 2016 by 8.48pm
cv http://scienceblogs.com Cited 20th July, 2016 by 8.48pm
cvi www.web.mit.edu/invent The Lemelson-MIT Program recognizes outstanding inventors, encourages sustainable new

solutions to real-world problems, and enables and inspires young people to pursue creative lives and careers through invention. Cited 13th July, 2016 by 3.12pm.

cvii www.web.mit.edu/invent Cited 13th July, 2016 by 2.30pm.

cviii www.web.mit.edu/invent Cited 13th July, 2016 by 2.31pm.

cixhttp://www.american.edu/training/ april-6-quotes-on-creativity-scb-2.pdf HR's Workplace Learning and Development Team, the AU Innovation Facilities and the Center for Teaching, research and Learning. Cited 13th July, 2016 by 4.32pm.

cx http://www.american.edu/training/ april-6-quotes-on-creativity-scb-2.pdf HR's Workplace Learning and Development Team, the AU Innovation Facilities and the Center for Teaching, research and Learning. Cited 13th July, 2016 by 4.32pm.

cxi In the Niger Delta, Nigeria where Gas and crude oil is explored, gas flare gets off the air as waste.

cxii http://www.american.edu/training/ april-6-quotes-on-creativity-scb-2.pdf HR's Workplace Learning and Development Team, the AU Innovation Facilities and the Center for Teaching, research and Learning. Cited 13th July, 2016 by 4.32pm.

cxiii http://5jscollingwood.weebly.com Cited 7th July, 2016 by 11.30pm

cxiv http://www.achievement.org Cited 7th July, 2016 by 11.30pm

cxv Microsoft Encarta. History Timeline, 2009.

cxvi http://www.wgu.edu/blogpost/improve-online-study-environment Cited 7th July, 2016 by 8.30pm

cxvii http://www.wikihow.com/Make-a-Study-Space Cited 6th July, 2016 by 12.30pm

cxviii A+ Research & Writing for high school and college students was created by Kathryn L. Schwartz - The iSchool at Drexel, College of Information Science and Technology, with major support from the College of Information at Florida State University. Initial donations provided by Intel and Sun Microsystems. Copyright Notice (c) 1995 - 2008 The Regents of the University of Michigan. All rights reserved. (c) 2009 - 2012, Drexel University.

cxix University of Illinois at Urbana-Champaign. Evaluating internet sources. Retrieved May 9, 2013, from http://www.bc.edu/libraries/help/howdoi/howto/evaluateinternet.html 2012. Cited 7th July, 2016 by 7.30pm

cxx www.aut.acnz/student-learning Cited 7th July, 2016 by 7.30pm

cxxi www.aut.acnz/student-learning Cited 7th July, 2016 by 7.30pm

cxxii University of Berkeley. Critical evaluation of resources. Retrieved May 9, 2013, from http://www.lib.berkeley.edu/instruct/guides/evaluation.html 2009. Cited 7th July, 2016 by 7.30pm

cxxiii www.aut.acnz/student-learning Cited 7th July, 2016 by 11.30pm

cxxiv Boston College Universities Library (n.d.). How do I evaluate internet resources. Retrieved May 9, 2013, from http://www.bc.edu/libraries/help/howdoi/howto/evaluateinternet.html Cited 6th July, 2016 by 1.28pm

cxxv http://www.wgu.edu/blogpost/improve-online-study-environment Cited 6th July, 2016 by 1.30pm

cxxvi www.aut.acnz/student-learning Cited 6th July, 2016 by 1.35pm

cxxvii Burg, B., Gilroy, S., Heath, K., Herron, J., John, T., Orbán, K. &. Zakarin, B. Writing with internet sources: a guide for Harvard Students. Cambridge, M.A.: Expository Writing Program Harvard College, 2007.

cxxviii http://www.learningcommons.uoguelph.ca Cited 7th July, 2016 by 10.30pm

cxxix Online Google Dictionary

cxxx Allen Olatunde. Career Choice Made Easy. Abeokuta: Africa! GLOW Missions Connect, 2015.

cxxxi Allen Olatunde. Career Choice Made Easy. Abeokuta: Africa! GLOW Missions Connect, 2015.

cxxxii Microsoft Encarta 2009

cxxxiii Microsoft Encarta 2009.

cxxxiv It is a biblical name of a harlot who lured a great warrior, Samson, into fornication in order to capture him for enemies' revenge. Delilah represents prostitution and seduction of any form from female persons just to pull down. Delilah's lap is the environment that promotes sexual immorality that men must run and flee away; for no spirituality can defeat it unless you flee.

cxxxv http://www.abort73.com/testimony/2262/ It was submitted to www.abort73.com by an 18-year-old woman on June 22, 2016. Cited 7th July, 2016 by 12.30pm

cxxxvi http://www.experienceproject.com/stories/Am-A-Teen-Mom/2796418 Cited 30th July, 2016 by 9.13pm

cxxxvii Kibui Francis. Precious Things Are Hidden. Posted on Facebook wall on March 1, 2015. www.facebook.com Cited 7th July, 2016 by 11.30pm

cxxxviii 1Corinthians 6:19-20

cxxxix Ahmad Muhammad Auwal. http://www.dailytrust.com.ng indecent dressing on campuses. Posted on January 29. 2015 4:00am. Cited on 7th July, 2016 by 12.25pm

cxl http://theinknewspaper.blogspot.com.ng/2015/01/indecent-dressing-among-students-in.html Blog of THE INK Newspaper- Uyo, Akwa Ibom State. Cited 7th July, 2016 by 12.30pm

cxli Aminah Oyeleye and Seliat Lawalon. Indecent dressing: A social malady? Posted on December 06, 2012 http://thenationonlineng.net/indecent-dressing-a-social-malady/ Cited on 10th July, 2016 by 1.18pm.

cxlii I said convincingly because of my experience in my tertiary institution days. Serious female students excelled more than boys. Their commitment to excellence was superb because they had few or no friends. They were not fashion-driven but book-driven.

cxliii D. Boyd and Ellison, N. Social Networking Sites: Definition, History, and Scholarship. Retrieved June 26, 2011, from Journal of Computer Mediated Communication: http://jcmc.indiana.edu/vol13/issue1/boyd.ellison.html 2007. Cited on 10th July, 2016 by 2.15pm.

cxliv S. Rose. Social Networking Addiction: Do you need detox from Facebook and twitter? (2009, August 2). Retrieved July 28, 2011, from http://www.associatedcontent.com/article/2014392/social_networking_addiction_pg3.html?cat=72 Cited on 10th July, 2016 by 2.18pm.

cxlv When I was in Ilorin around 2012, I had this scenario. It was funny experience to see an undergraduate shedding tears for faulty phone just because there will be breach on her chat lifestyle.

cxlvi https://www.researchgate.net/researcher/81488295_I_A_Ajayi Ajayi et al., 2010
cxlvii Rotimi, Adewale. Violence in the Citadel: The Menace of Secret Cults in the Nigerian Universities PDF, Nordic Journal of African Studies 14(1): 79–98 (2005)
cxlviii www.wikipedia.com
cxlix www.wikipedia.com
cl Samson Erughe. Effects of Cultism on Campuses. Post on February 14, 2015 http://www.nigerianobservernews.com/2015/02/effects-cultism-campuses/ cited on 1.11pm 13th July, 2016
cli http://www.who.int/mental_health/management/depression/definition/en/ Last accessed January 5, 2010 cited on 1.15pm 13th July, 2016
clii John Dallard and Neal E. Miller. Personality and Psychotherapy: An Analysis in Terms of Learning, Thinking and Culture. McGraw-Hill, New York, 1950.
cliii http://www.medicinenet.com
cliv http://www.uky.edu/~eushe2/Pajares/OnFailingG.html
clv http://www.onlinecollege.org/2010/02/16/50-famously-successful-people-who-failed-at-first/
clvi http://www.uky.edu/~eushe2/Pajares/OnFailingG.html
clvii Peale, Vincent Norman. You Can If You Think You Can. UK: The Random House Group Limited, 1974.
clviii Michael Catt. Courageous Living: Dare to Take a Stand. Nashville: B & H Publishing Group, 2011.
clix My son's experience in 2013 at Minna, Nigeria
clx 2 Kings 7:6-7
clxi My exit as an Associate Pastor at Zion Baptist Church, Minna, Nigeria in October, 2014
clxii Microsoft Encarta 2009. Microsoft Corporation, 1993-2008
clxiii Microsoft Encarta Dictionary 2009. Microsoft Corporation, 1993-2008.
clxiv Bill Klemm. Sharp Brains. May 14, 2009. 8 Tips To Remember What You Read http://sharpbrains.com/blog/2009/05/14/8-tips-to-remember-what-you-read/
clxv Democratic president of Nigeria 2016
clxvi www.linkedin.com/pulse/words-drben-carson-kusasira-elliot posted by Kusasira Elliot September 18, 2015, cited on 13th July, 2016 by 6.33pm.
clxvii Myles Munroe was a Bahamian Evangelical Christian Evangelist and ordained Pentecostal minister who founded the Bahamas Faith Ministries International. He authored books on leadership and purpose. He was an inspirational and motivational speaker. He died in an auto crash accident on his personal plane on 9th November, 2014.
clxviii Vincent Norman Peale. You Can If You Think You Can. UK: The Random House Group Limited, 1974.
clxix Luke 23:34
clxx Vincent Norman Peale. You Can If You Think You Can. UK: The Random House Group Limited, 1974.
clxxi Matthew 11:28; Colossians 2:14-15; 2 Corinthians 5:17
clxxii Vincent Norman Peale. You Can If You Think You Can. UK: The Random House Group Limited, 1974.
clxxiii Vincent Norman Peale. You Can If You Think You Can. UK: The Random House Group Limited, 1974.
clxxiv Vincent Norman Peale. You Can If You Think You Can. UK: The Random House Group Limited, 1974.
clxxv Vincent Norman Peale. You Can If You Think You Can. UK: The Random House Group Limited, 1974.
clxxvi Bimbo Odukoya. How to Handle Rejection. Lagos: Grace Springs Africa Publishers, 2006.
clxxvii Ephesians 6:12
clxxviii 2 Corinthians 10:3
clxxix Colossians 1:16
clxxx Philippians 2:10
clxxxi Matthew 11:12
clxxxii Matthew 16:19
clxxxiii Allen Olatunde. When I Seek God's Face. Minna: aiconcept, 2013.
clxxxiv Allen Olatunde. When I Seek God's Face. Minna: aiconcept, 2013.
clxxxv 1 Peter 5:7
clxxxvi Philippians 4:6-7
clxxxvii Proverbs 23:7
clxxxviii Luke 6:45
clxxxix Luke 6:38
cxc Discovery Channel on cable around late December, 2015
cxci Psalm 14:1
cxcii Daniel 4:30-37
cxciii Isaiah 45:9
cxciv Isaiah 29:16
cxcv Isaiah 40:28
cxcvi Daniel 2:19-20
cxcvii Job 28:20; 28
cxcviii Jeremiah 9:23-24
cxcix Microsoft Encarta 2009. Microsoft Corporation, 1993-2008
cc Jeremiah 29:11
cci Jeremiah 31:17a
ccii Genesis 37:5
cciii Genesis 37:9a

cciv Jim Rohn. S.M.A.R.T Goals. America: Jim Rohn International. www.appleseeds.org/rohn_smart-goalshtm Cited 2nd August, 2016 by 10.25pm.

ccv Chinese Proverbs

ccvi Vincent Norman Peale. You Can If You Think You Can. UK: The Random House Group Limited, 1974.

ccvii Allen Olatunde. Career Choice Made Easy. Abeokuta: Africa! GLOW Missions Connect, 2015.

ccviii Philippians 4:13

ccix Microsoft Encarta 2009. ©1993-2008 Microsoft Corporation.

ccx Vincent Norman Peale. You Can If You Think You Can. UK: The Random House Group Limited, 1974.

ccxi Michael Catt. Courageous Living: Dare to Take a Stand. Nashville: B & H Publishing Group, 2011.

ccxii Allen Olatunde. When I Seek God's Face. Minna: aiconcept, 2013.

ccxiii Esther 4:16

ccxiv Michael Catt. Courageous Living: Dare to Take a Stand. Nashville: B & H Publishing Group, 2011.

ccxv Michael Catt. Courageous Living: Dare to Take a Stand. Nashville: B & H Publishing Group, 2011.

ccxvi Allen Olatunde. When I Seek God's Face. Minna: aiconcept, 2013.

ccxvii Michael Catt. Courageous Living: Dare to Take a Stand. Nashville: B & H Publishing Group, 2011.

ccxviii Press Pass. The Annual Newsletter for Candidates of the Unified Tertiary Matriculation Examinations. Vol. 2, UTME, 2014.

ccxix Lloyd John Ogilvie. Lord of the Impossible. Nashville: Abingdon, 1984. 99

ccxx Michael Catt. Courageous Living: Dare to Take a Stand. Nashville: B & H Publishing Group, 2011.

ccxxi Michael Catt. Courageous Living: Dare to Take a Stand. Nashville: B & H Publishing Group, 2011.

ccxxii C. H. Spurgeon. Sermon on Men of the Old Testament. Grand rapids: Zondervan, nd, 131.

ccxxiii My experience in year 2004 during WAEC at Ijaiye Grammar School, Ijaiye, Oyo State when I wrote exam to make up my result

ccxxiv Proverbs 22:29

ccxxv John 9:4

ccxxvi Philippians 2:13

ccxxvii Newell S. Booth. This is Africa South of the Sahara. New York: Friendship Press, 1945.

ccxxviii www.premiumtimesng.com/regional/nwest/197855-sokoto-car-designer-gets-scholarship-study-u-s.html

ccxxix www.servantmedia.com.ng/?p=2800

ccxxx Newell S. Booth. This is Africa South of the Sahara. New York: Friendship Press, 1945.

ccxxxi Newell S. Booth. This is Africa South of the Sahara. New York: Friendship Press, 1945.

ccxxxii Newell S. Booth. This is Africa South of the Sahara. New York: Friendship Press, 1945.

ccxxxiii Ohadike, Don C. Sacred Drums of Liberation: Religious and Music of Resistance in Africa and the Diaspora. Asmara, Eritrea: Africa World Press, 2007.

ccxxxiv Ulack, Richard. "Malaysia." Microsoft Encarta 2009 [DVD]. Redmond, WA: Microsoft Corporation, 2008.

ccxxxv Vincent Obia. One Year After Buhari shifts Ground on Key Economic Issues. This Day Online Newspaper, May 29, 2016. It was cited on 16th July, 2016 by 944.pm.

ccxxxvi IT Vessel at Ilorin www.itvessel.com

ccxxxvii http://listernaija.com/wp-content/uploads/2016/01/the-nigerian-who-designed-an-american-car.jpg?8a7265

ccxxxviii Http://itvessel.com

ccxxxix http://listernaija.com/wp-content/uploads/2016/01/Saleh-Shehu-balami.jpg?8a7265

ccxl http://linkedin.com/pulse/make-india-outsourcing-your-customized-web-mobile-desktop-trivedi

ccxli William J. Clinton. Public Papers of the Presidents of the United State of America, 2000. 1358

ccxlii http://linkedin.com/pulse/make-india-outsourcing-your-customized-web-mobile-desktop-trivedi

ccxliii http://en.m.wikipedia.org/wiki/salisu_buhari

ccxliv Chinedu Arizona-Ogwu. Doctored Certificates: The Undervalue of Education in Nigeria http://nigeriansinamerica.com cited 17th July, 2016 by 6.38pm.

ccxlv Lord Acton (1834 - 1902). British historian, April 3, 1887.Often misquoted as "Power corrupts..." Letter to Bishop Mandell Creighton. Microsoft Encarta 2009.

ccxlvi William Pitt the Elder (1708 - 1778). British prime minister. Speech to the House of Lords, the upper house of the British Parliament.

ccxlvii Matthew 24:28

ccxlviii Sam Adeyemi. Multiply Your Success Lead. Lagos: Pneuma Publishing Ltd, 2009.

ccxlix Gbile Akanni. Oracles for Leaders: God's Principles for an Enduring Rule. Gboko: Peace House Publications, 2009.

ccl Nehemiah 4:1-23

ccli Michael Catt. Courageous Living: Dare to Take a Stand. Nashville: B & H Publishing Group, 2011.

cclii 2 Peter 2:14-18

ccliii Proverbs 1:7

ccliv "Sani Abacha." Microsoft Encarta 2009 [DVD]. Redmond, WA: Microsoft Corporation, 2008.

cclv www.biography.com/people/muammar-al-gaddafi-39014 cited 17th July, 2016 by 8.04pm.

cclvi Newitt, Malyn D. D. "Robert Mugabe." Microsoft Encarta 2009 [DVD]. Redmond, WA: Microsoft Corporation, 2008.

cclvii www.en.wikipedia.org/wiki/aliko_dangote cited 17th July, 2016 by 9.23pm.

cclviii Taiwo Ogunmola. Nigeria: Casualization of Workers is Inhuman – Etafo. An interview with Augustine Etafo, the National President of Construction and Civil Engineering Senior Staff (CCESSA) www.allafrica.com/stories/201105240964.html cited 17th July, 2016 by 9.23pm.

cclix Jesse Oluwapelumi Adesina. Career Talk. A discussion class on career talk at Patterson Memorial Baptist grammar school, Abeokuta on 21s July, 2016 around 1.00pm.

[cclx] Interview with medical workers , Dr. Adenike Odewanbi (NMA Chairman Abeokuta Chapter) and Dr. Kunle Ashimi of Federal Medical Center, Idi-aba Abeokuta on the strike actions at the hospital interviewed by Citizen Forum on Rock City FM Radio, Abeokuta on 1st March, 2016 by 9.29am.

[cclxi] Arukaino Umukoro. Our daughter's journey of no return to India – Parents of 26-year-old ago died during surgery in Indian hospital. Headline on Punch Newspaper published on 8th May, 2016 and cited on 30 July, 2016 by 6.19pm.

[cclxii] "Research and Development." Microsoft Encarta 2009 [DVD]. Redmond, WA: Microsoft Corporation, 2008.

[cclxiii] Stock, Robert. "Nigeria." Microsoft® Encarta® 2009 [DVD]. Redmond, WA: Microsoft Corporation, 2008.

[cclxiv] "Ben Okri." Microsoft® Encarta® 2009 [DVD]. Redmond, WA: Microsoft Corporation, 2008.

[cclxv] "Ben Okri." Microsoft® Encarta® 2009 [DVD]. Redmond, WA: Microsoft Corporation, 2008.

[cclxvi] Dobson. James C. When God Doesn't Make Sense. Focus on the Family Australia, Tyndale House Publishers, February 2009.

[cclxvii] Psalm 139:13-17

[cclxviii] Psalm 139:1-4

[cclxix] 1 Kings 3:7-9

[cclxx] James 1:5

[cclxxi] Proverb 8:11-36

[cclxxii] Proverbs 3:5-8

[cclxxiii] J.P. Moreland. Love Your God With All Our Mind Leader's Guide. 5501 Independence Pkwy. Suite 100. Plano, TX 75023. www.gradresources.org A pdf articles downloaded on 30th July, 2016 by 8.34pm

[cclxxiv] Galatians 4:19

[cclxxv] John 3:30

9 789785 089257